A Passion for Cigars

FIFTH AVENUE · NEW YORK

Nat Sherman

INTERNATIONAL

NAT SHERMAN'S

A Passion for Cigars

*Selecting, Preserving,
Smoking, and Savoring
One of Life's Greatest Pleasures*

JOEL SHERMAN

President and Chief Executive Officer, Nat Sherman, Incorporated

WITH ROBERT IVRY

Andrews and McMeel

A Universal Press Syndicate Company

KANSAS CITY

Produced by The Philip Lief Group, Inc.

Library of Congress Cataloging-in-Publication Data

Nat Sherman's a passion for cigars: selecting, preserving, smoking, and savoring one of life's greatest pleasures / by Joel Sherman.

    p. cm.
Includes bibliographical references and index.
ISBN 0-8362-2182-6
    1. Cigars. 2. Cigar industry. I. Sherman, Joel. II. Ivry, Robert. III. Nat Sherman Incorporated.
TS2260.N38 1996
394.1'4–dc20   96-9189
                                                        CIP

First Printing, October 1996
Second Printing, November 1996

Grateful acknowledgment for photographs is made to the following:

The Library of Congress, page 32; The Key West Art and Historical Society, page 16; the Tampa-Hillsborough County Public Library System, page 17, 23, and 54; and the University of South Florida Library Special Collections, page 19.

All other photographs and illustrations generously provided courtesy of Nat Sherman, Inc.

Recipes courtesy of the Culinary Institute of America.

Book design, maps on pages 57, 62, 63, and 65, and typesetting by Martin Lubin Graphic Design.

Color insert photographs by John Carriglio of Camart Studios.

Acknowledgments

To say that this book would not have been possible without the work, sweat and toil of thousands of farmers, growers, sorters and makers in all the many regions of the world where tobacco grows, would be an understatement. To ignore their passion and love of product would be an injustice.

And certainly to Ramon and Henry, Alfonse and David, Bunny and Eddie, Frank and Sol and the many others from whom I learned and developed my passion by dint of exposure, osmosis and toil, for the knowledge they have shared with me through word and deed, I shall always be grateful. For Bob Ivry's patience and persistence eclipsed only by the prodding and organizing of my wonderful, respected, loved and too often "taken for granted" assistant Helene.

To my children William, Michele and Laurence who now share this passion for our industry with me with a special extra thanks to William, who put so much effort into the details of this book. Finally and most of all, to my wife, Myrna, who has tolerated my mistress tobacco and allowed our children to go down this path of passion with me.

Contents

A sixteen-page color insert follows page 64.

Introduction

Cigar smoking is one of life's greatest pleasures. After forty-five years in the business, I still find cigar smoking an absolute romance, a sensual and deeply personal experience. I was asked to write this book because I'm considered an expert–I started in the tobacco trade as a counter clerk and stock boy for my father, Nat, in his retail store in Manhattan, which he opened in 1930, and I now run the store and an international mail-order business as president of Nat Sherman Incorporated. I've personally been involved in the years of development of our current catalog of eight different cigar blends available in over forty different sizes, as well as the selection and marketing of scores of accessory products. But I don't expect you to be impressed by that, for one simple reason–and that reason is the most important point I wish to make to you, the reader: When it comes to choosing a good cigar, there's only one expert, and that's you!

People in the cigar trade will try to dictate the right cigar for you and the wrong one, but in the end they're just blowing smoke. There's always been a terrific amount of myth in the cigar business, some of it silly and harmless, most of it counterproductive and just plain false. Almost all of it comes from somebody trying to sell you something. These days, owing to the recent surge in the popularity of the premium-quality product, just about anyone who's smoked a cigar and read a book about them is trying to cash in by passing himself off as an expert. They rely

---

Cigar smoking is an absolute romance, a sensual and deeply personal experience.

---

on the current vogue and the conventional wisdom, and they can often steer you wrong. I've spent forty-five years building relationships in the business, all the way from growers and manufacturers to the many customers who frequent our retail store, but what I offer you is simply advice. I leave the judgment to you. It breaks my heart to hear of people who love inexpensive, machine-made, short-filled cigars and won't smoke them because they're not the "in" thing right now, or because some so-called expert tells them they're not any good. It's a shame.

For this reason, I'm against ratings systems, and you won't find me telling anyone in this book what to smoke and what not to smoke. Hanging a number on a cigar, or giving a certain number of stars to rate cigars, is a practice I don't much care for. I will, however, make it easier for you to navigate through the wonderful world of cigars and find your perfect cigar companion. In these pages, I'll share my love for cigars and my extensive knowledge of them, but the final choice will be yours.

When it comes to choosing the right cigar, there's only one expert, and that's you!

And the choices today have never been better. The quality of the product has improved steadily over the years, and the variety available to today's smoker was unheard-of when I first started in the business in the early 1950s. The cigar smoker was a different type of person, too. Back then, men used to chew their cigars and smoke them one after the other. It was an aggressive, brutal thing–a dirty habit. Maybe that was indicative of the times or the lifestyles of the men who smoked cigars, I don't know. But today cigar smoking is associated more with leisure, with those few minutes of respite in the middle of a hectic day, or that mellow hour after dinner–with moments of calm in an otherwise crazy world. Today, like millions of other people, I smoke a cigar to slow myself down. I like to sit in my

Joel Sherman

library with a glass of port or sherry and enjoy a book while I smoke. Smoking doesn't cloud the mind—rather, it clarifies things and allows rare insight in contemplation, providing a center of sanity and peace.

As enjoyable as a cigar can be when smoked in solitude, I find it just as refreshing to smoke one in the company of others who also enjoy this pastime. I know of no other thing in the world that better symbolizes camaraderie. Cigars are celebratory and fun; they signify special events; they are tokens of generosity and cheer. Cigars, too, are great equalizers. If a boss offers an employee a cigar and they light up together, social position and class distinctions suddenly are forgotten, and the room is filled with good fellowship. Why does this happen? I'm not sure.

The upsurge in the popularity of the cigar has made smoking them more acceptable, even in places where a short time ago NO SMOKING signs were hung. In the same spirit, smokers ought to practice common courtesy in the presence of nonsmokers. Cigar smoking is not an in-your-face operation, it's a "Will you join me?"

I believe in freedom of choice, and I believe it ought to include not only the decision of whether or not to smoke, but what to smoke—down to the single, specific cigar. One thing I try to impress upon the salespeople at my store is this: When a customer asks for a certain brand, take the box out of the showcase and allow him to choose which one he wants. Some customers will say, "You pick one for me," but to me, that's like having the guy who works in the produce department choose your tomatoes for you. I believe that each cigar has a distinct vibration. I know this because I expe-

---

There's a terrific amount of myth in the cigar business, some of it fun, most of it just plain wrong.

---

rience it every day. With literally thousands of cigars at my disposal, I still find that one of the toughest decisions I have to make is: What cigar will I smoke? Once I've chosen a variety and a size and narrowed the preference to a particular box, I want the freedom to decide on the specific cigar. It's part of the enjoyment of cigar smoking. One cigar out of all the ones in the box will speak to me. It reaches out and appeals to all my senses. Is it the coloration, the way the light hits it, the vein or lack of vein in the wrapper? I don't know for sure, but I know it looks good to me, and I'll smoke it. It goes back to personal choice, an aesthetic judgment that each individual must make for himself or herself, and that's a big part of the subtle essence of cigar enjoyment.

I think by now it's evident that I love cigars. I love the tobacco leaf itself, so moist and fragile and full of possibility. I love the industry, the people who grow the tobacco, the pickers, the tenders, the curers, the rollers, the pack-

The conventional wisdom is worthless.

ers and shippers, the retail workers, the panache and romance of the product we develop and sell. When you look at how much labor and love and care go into producing a single cigar, how much of it must be done by hand by highly skilled workers, it's got to be one of the greatest bargains in the world. Though I don't think the price should be any higher, a hand-made, good-quality cigar under ten dollars is an incredible buy when you think about all the work and care and history that has gone into it.

It's my affection for the industry and my passion for the product that has compelled me to write this book. In the following pages, I'll outline the highlights of the history of the cigar in order to help deepen your appreciation of it; sketch out the extensive journey tobacco goes through to become a premium cigar; share my knowledge about the many varieties of cigars, to help you choose which one is best for you; provide some tips on keeping your cigars in top condition; give you ideas for putting on a cigar dinner; and point you in the right direction if you care to find the best places to buy cigars. Along the way, I hope some of my enthusiasm for cigars rubs off, and some of my fascination, which remains strong even after more than four decades in the business.

My father once said that if you teach your children all you know, they won't know any more than you do. It is my hope that this book will help educate and fire the imagination of a new generation who's discovered cigar smoking–one of the greatest pleasures in life.

Chapter One

The History of Cigars:
Columbus to Clinton

The cigar you hold in your hand today is a small piece of the history of the world. Not only is it the result of the devoted work of many generations of people who were passionate about the art of cigar making and were dedicated to its refinement and perfection, it tells the tale of America itself, spanning the centuries before Columbus, colonial times, war, the industrial revolution, and the age of technology. What other manufactured product boasts so much modern polish, yet was so simply elegant in its conception that it functions virtually the same as it did a thousand years ago? And cigars are as American as you can get. Tobacco, baseball, and jazz are this country's three unique gifts, embraced around the globe. Cigars not only link the New World with the Old, they stand as a very symbol of the good life that has always been an American promise.

More precious than gold

Myth and romance have fueled tobacco's mystique since the very beginning, though nobody knows exactly when that beginning was. When Columbus landed in what is now the heart of the world's cigar-making center in 1492, the Caribbean natives had been using tobacco for centuries, and the Europeans were shocked to find them "drinking smoke" out of cigars that measured two to three feet long. They'd never seen anything like it. Though rumor had it that Columbus didn't like tobacco much himself, it didn't take long for its popularity to extend to most of Europe, and Spain ended up earning more riches from its early monopoly on cigars than it did from the main object of its conquests—gold.

Spain earned more money from tobacco than it did from gold.

There are competing theories as to how tobacco got its name. While the Taino Indians of the West Indies called it *cohiba*–now the name of a famous brand of Cuban cigar that Fidel Castro himself would give as gifts to visiting dignitaries–other tribes throughout the New World referred to it as *uppowoc, petum,* and *piecetl.* But it seems– like America itself–the name "tobacco" was a misnomer that stuck. Forty-three years after Columbus's maiden landing, Gonzalo Fernández de Oviedo, the Spanish viceroy of Santo Domingo, wrote that the Indians "employed a tube, shaped like a Y, inserting the forked extremities in their nostrils and the tube itself in the lighted weed.... Those who could not procure the right sort of wood took their smoke through a hollow reed; it is this the Indians called 'toba-go,' not the weeds or its effects, as some have supposed."

Those early cigars must have been very harsh. The tobacco plant was much cruder back then–cultivation and careful breeding have made the leaf we smoke today a lot mellower. Sometimes the Indians rolled up their greenish tobacco in palm leaves or dried maize strips, and for some unknown reason they soaked their cigars in seawater before they smoked them. That had to add a kick.

Columbus described these Indian cigars as a "roll of leaves in a leaf of itself"–by an odd coincidence almost exactly how cigars are described in today's Internal Revenue Service regulations!

"Eureka!" cried the garbage collector

Since tobacco leaves must be aged before they're fit for smoking, it's something of a mystery how the Indians started the practice. It's possible they stumbled upon it by accident when they burned stacks of the drying plant meant for compost. If that's true, credit a Mayan garbage collector with being the first person ever to enjoy a good smoke. He must have liked it and told his friends, because the practice

The history of cigars is the history of America.

spread, and the first Europeans in the West Indies reported seeing Indians inhale tobacco smoke from burning piles of leaves. Smoking the raw, uncured tobacco in that manner took a certain amount of courage and a favorable wind direction. I'll stick to cigars.

Many smokers nowadays would call their relationship with cigars a religious one, but Native American cultures took it a step further and made tobacco part of their ritual ceremonies. Tobacco is still used today by Indians as an offering to deities, and smoke was blown in the faces of young warriors to stir up their courage before battle. The Mayans of Mexico and Central America, who are credited with being history's first tobacco smokers, painted pictures of their gods smoking cigars and mixed

---

Myth and romance have fueled tobacco's mystique since the very beginning.

their tobacco with hallucinogenic substances for a little extra inspiration. In the old days, just like today, tobacco was used to seal deals—it was common for Native Americans to pass the peace pipe, called a calumet, to mark such occasions.

The origin of the word "cigar" is cloaked in mystery, too. The Mayans, who invented the cigar, are said to have called it *sik'ar*, and the Spanish appropriated the term and added a Latin lilt, making it *cigarro*. Because cigarro resembles the Spanish word for cicada—*cigarra*—some so-called experts have tried to make the etymological-entomological connection by saying that those old Spaniards must have thought their cigars looked like the insect, but I'm skeptical. Anyone who's tried to light up a cicada knows there's no comparison.

The Spanish began the extensive exporting of cigars to Europe soon after they conquered Cuba in 1515. Forty-five years later, the French ambassador to Spain and Portugal took tobacco seeds north to France, and the craze quickly caught on in the rest of Western Europe and the world. His name was Jean Nicot, and he gave us the word "nicotine." Soon, tobacco was being grown all over the globe—in Russia, Ceylon (now Sri Lanka), Java, and the Philippines. Though for centuries the English and French preferred pipes to cigars, the Dutch were quick to jump on the cigar bandwagon, and many took up cultivation of cigar tobacco when they settled in the New World. While cigarette- and pipe-tobacco plantations flourished in the Virginia and Carolina colonies, the Dutch were responsible for establishing the first great center of cigar-tobacco growing in America, in Massachusetts, starting as early as 1610.

Daguerrotype of an unknown man with a cigar, mid-nineteenth century.

Bands for dandies

It seems that little about the history of the cigar is free from myth, and controversy also surrounds the origin of the cigar band. I subscribe to the notion that the first cigar bands were used because wrapper leaves on the typical Dutch-made cigars of the seventeenth century were rough and discolored and not so easy on the eyes. Because cigar makers wanted to sell a more attractive cigar, they'd mask the wrapper's irregularities by dipping the cigar in a cosmetic powder made of tobacco dust and water. This powder made the cigar look spiffy and the color of its wrapper leaf more uniform, but it rubbed off easily when the cigar was handled. Though it wasn't too difficult to wipe the powder off the lips, the hands–especially ones wearing the white gloves that were popular among smokers at the time–would get stained. Bands were put around the cigar to spare dandies the embarrassment of tobacco-colored soil marks on their gloved fingers. Some ingenious manufacturer decided that it would be advantageous to identify his brand on the band, and voilà! a new art form was born. Since the bands functioned as distinctive brand-name identifiers, they outlasted the practice of coating cigars with the cosmetic powder.

Cigar bands protected the white-gloved fingers of European dandies.

Cigar boxes adorned with their famous, elaborate brand-name identification had to wait until 1837, however, when Cuban cigar manufacturer Ramón Allones, an immigrant from France, became the first tobacconist in history to use a full-colored label. To this day, his name graces a top-quality line of cigars.

Though tobacco cultivation was in full swing in the American colonies as early as the beginning of the 1600s, the first imported cigar didn't arrive on these shores until 1762. That year, a British naval officer named Colonel Israel Putnam was a hero in Britain's successful pacification and brief one-year occupation of Cuba. "Old Put"–who later became an American general in the Revolutionary War–was rewarded with as many Cuban cigars as he could carry home. Not only did his overburdened donkeys make their way back to Putnam's home in Pomfret, Connecticut, with the first Havana cigars ever seen in what was soon to become the United States, they carried Cuban tobacco as well, perhaps giving Connecticut its head start in the cigar-tobacco industry.

Financing the Revolution

Americans of the current generation who want to restrict smokers' rights may have forgotten that our country was built and sustained for years on the strength of the tobacco industry. Benjamin Franklin financed the Continental Congresses by swinging a loan from France based on tobacco futures, and the "royal leaf" virtually paid for the American Revolution.

Tobacco virtually paid for the American Revolution.

Though my father, Nat Sherman, would've loved to take credit for opening this country's first cigar store, a German immigrant did it before him, setting up shop in Lancaster, Pennsylvania, in 1770–a few years before Nat's

Women workers in an Ybor City cigar factory, 1929. The tradition of women cigar rollers began in earnest in the nineteenth century and has continued to this day. Ybor City's heyday wasn't as long-lived, but at the time this photo was taken, that famous section of Tampa, Florida, was enjoying a colossal pre-Depression boom in the sales of handmade cigars.

time. And those curmudgeons who still hold to the archaic belief that cigar smoking should be restricted to men would do well to remember that the entire domestic cigar-making industry was started by a woman in 1801.

Known only as the wife of an East Windsor, Connecticut, farmer named Prout, she couldn't understand why her husband exported his tobacco crop to the West Indies, where it was rolled into cigars and shipped back for sale in Connecticut. In the proud American tradition of cutting out the middleman, she hired a team of neighbor women, who began rolling the cigars themselves. By 1870, Connecticut alone boasted two hundred thirty-five cigar factories, and to this day, the state produces some of the best wrapper tobacco in the world.

In the early 1800s, just three major varieties of cigar were available to American smokers. They were "long nines" (pencil-thin), "short sixes" (stubby), and "supers" (shaped like modern cigars, but twisted at the ends instead of gummed together). "Short sixes" were handed out free in taverns to steady customers—they were thought to whet the thirst for beer—and the regular price was two for a penny, or "two-fer." Don't think for a minute it was a bargain, though. A penny was a lot of money back then, because most purchases people made were by barter.

Birth of the "stogie"

Cigars of that era were not only a lot harsher than the ones we enjoy today, they were made of dry tobacco. Folks just didn't have the technology to keep their cigars moist, like Americans prefer to do now, so if someone ever tries to sell you an antique humidor, you're better off buying the Brooklyn Bridge. They just didn't have them. Starting in the 1840s, Pennsylvania became famous for its production of a dry and inexpensive, powerful and pungent cigar nicknamed the "stogie" because the makers used the famous Conestoga wagon, manufactured in the same region, as an advertising come-on. Some say the long, thin cigars resembled the spokes of a wheel from the Conestoga wagons, and that may be true, too. It was short-filled—meaning the inside of the cigar was filled with bits of tobacco, rather than a bunch of whole leaves—and the tobacco was all Pennsylvania-grown. Nowadays, tobaccos from different regions are blended and cross-bred to produce a finer, smoother smoke, and the all-Pennsylvania filler tobacco of that era is a distant memory. But that cigar remains famous because smokers shortened the name Conestoga to "stogie," and the moniker is still alive today, synonymous with lower-priced cigars.

In those days, since transportation was rustic, growers and rollers had to follow the westward migration of American settlers, and every fair-sized town had its own cigar makers. Tobacco farms dotted the Midwest and the West, and every ship that left the East Coast for California by way of Cape Horn held its stowage of barrels stuffed with cigars. The product was as popular then as it's ever been. In 1849, the year of the gold rush, the *New York Times* claimed that every day in New York more money was spent on cigars than bread.

Despite the difficulties in shipping, imported cigars were available in the larger U.S. cities–in 1840, for instance, thirteen million were brought in–and, though just as dry, their quality was said to have been much better than what the local farmers and merchants could supply.

Tampa rules

The mid-nineteenth century was a period of explosive growth in the domestic cigar industry–literally. After a fire destroyed his Key West factory in 1869, Vincente Martínez Ybor, a successful Cuban cigar manufacturer, moved north to what was then still the sleepy seaside hamlet of

Ybor City cigar factory, 1896. By the turn of the century, the cigar business had been flourishing in Tampa since Vincente Martínez Ybor moved his factory north from Key West 27 years earlier.

A factory explosion in Key West forced the U.S. cigar industry north to Tampa— and to worldwide fame.

Tampa, establishing an important enough business that his part of town was renamed Ybor City. Handmade cigars made in the Ybor City section of Tampa, using Cuban and other Caribbean tobaccos, became world renowned for the next one hundred years.

The cigar industry employed thousands of workers throughout the country as rollers, but Tampa was a paradise for these skilled craftspeople. While in New York City much of the cigar rolling was done as piecework by families living in tenements under horrible conditions, Tampa rollers were allowed to smoke all the cigars they liked, an old Spanish custom. When they left at the end of the day, they were given three free choice brands, a practice that was finally curtailed because of the tax money the companies still had to pay on these freebies. Expert rollers were considered artists and were treated well. They never had to "punch the clock"—they came and went as they pleased. Even with this special treatment, each of them worked hard enough and long enough to roll, on average, 30,000 cigars a year. Factories hired readers, who sat perched above the rolling floor and read newspapers, novels, philosophy, and, occasionally, incendiary political tracts, to the workers as they rolled. Readers in the Tampa factories were fired in 1931 after a bitter strike the owners claimed was fomented in part by what the readers chose to read to the workers. I don't know what those books were, but when the strike was over, radios had taken the readers' place.

"Only one cigar at a time" Famous Americans contributed to the mid-nineteenth-century boom in cigar use. The only time Mark Twain didn't have a cigar cradled between his fingers was when he slept; when questioned about his habit, he replied, "I smoke in moderation—only one cigar at a time." He was famous for filling the boxes of expensive, fancy cigars with the cheap, acrid variety he preferred and watching for his guests' reactions when they lit up. "To quit smoking is the easiest thing I ever did," he once said. "I ought to know because I've done it a thousand times." Civil War generals Ulysses S. Grant and William Tecumseh Sherman were also chain cigar smokers. General Sherman—no relation—never smoked his down to the end, though, and every day he left a row of half-smoked cigars on his desk, which became known as "Sherman's old soldiers." Cigars helped the Union win the bloody battle of Antietam. A Rebel officer used a piece of paper containing General Robert E. Lee's orders to bundle his cigars, and when the cigars fell into the hands of the Union soldiers, so did the Confederate battle plans.

This was the era of the cigar-store Indian. Though the first was carved in England and installed in front of a Boston tobacco shop in 1730, the 1870s saw their popularity skyrocket and more than 100,000 were believed to have been sold. Cigar shops also used statues of Scottish Highlanders, Turks, and Canadian trappers to publi-

---

"I only take one smoke a day," Mark Twain once said. "It commences in the morning and ends just before I go to bed."

---

cize their wares. These elaborate advertisements must have worked, because in 1890, one billion cigars were sold in the United States: average price, four cents.

Cigar stores in the 1880s were like gentlemen's clubs, with marble floors and brass cuspidors. All you had to do to join for an afternoon was buy a cigar. Since they were illuminated by gas, the shops were equipped with special devices attached to the counters with which you could light your cigar by a gas flame.

Victorian backlash

Smoking in public—and in front of ladies— was not only considered rude in those days, in some places it could land you in jail. In 1880, Boston passed an ordinance that made it illegal to smoke on the street. Facing that kind of condemnation, smokers took their pleasure indoors. Smoking rooms in hotels and smoking compartments on trains became the rage, and though cigars have always been the delight of the working man as much as the patrician of the upper crust, the image of courtly gentlemen dressed in silk smoking jackets and wearing tasseled fezzes congregating after dinner to share stories and fine cigars originated during this time. Yet the paragon of this era, Queen Victoria, was famous for her distaste of smoking. Legend has it that she forced anyone who dared light up in Windsor Castle to blow their smoke

---

In 1901, King Edward VII rang in the modern cigar era by proclaiming, "Gentlemen, you may smoke."

---

into the fireplace so it could waft out the chimney. Am I the only one who's reminded of Hillary Clinton when he hears this story?

When Victoria passed the torch to King Edward VII, so to speak, in 1901, the legendary smoking lamp was lit. "Gentlemen, you may smoke," the king said, and millions did—and still do. By the Second World War, King Edward was the highest-selling brand of cigars in the world and, now made in Florida, it remains one of the most popular to this day.

To feed the early twentieth century's unprecedented expansion of the cigar business, the industry underwent a rapid mechanization in its first decades. In 1910, nearly twenty-three thousand U.S. factories produced mostly handmade cigars, but by 1929, because of mechanization, there were only six thousand cigar factories left. They pumped out more product, however. In 1907, Americans smoked four billion cigars; that number doubled by 1929.

With the twentieth century came the advent of the humidified cigar. Until then, smokers were content to puff on dry local brands, which were sold in shops that gave absolutely no heed to the need for cigars to be maintained in a humid, warm environment.

The Cuban mystique

Until the twentieth century, the greatest innovations the manufacturers of stogies and nickel cigars could come up with was the beautiful designs on the boxes in which the cigars were sold. There was no creativity in the making of the cigars themselves, no experimentation in new tastes or shapes, no marketing of national brands, and very little American access to the finer tobaccos being grown in the Caribbean. All that changed in the 1920s. That's when Cuba, which throughout its colonial history had been sheltered by an overprotective imperial Spain, finally opened up—mostly to gamblers and rumrunners—and the mystique of the Cuban cigar spread from the Havana casinos by way of the gangster. The high rollers and the fancy Dans drove

Florida State Fair exhibit, 1937. An embargo on trade with Cuba was the furthest thing from anyone's mind!

the swankiest cars, drank the smoothest bathtub gin, wore the nattiest clothes, had the best-looking women—and they smoked the big, high-priced Cuban cigars. Nicknamed "Havanas," they cost a buck in an era when the average Joe was being told—by Woodrow Wilson's vice president, Thomas Riley Marshall—that "what this country needs is a good five-cent cigar." The average Joe may have needed a good five-cent cigar, but he saw Al Capone on the newsreels and Edward G. Robinson in the feature films smoking that masterpiece of Cuban design, and he wanted to smoke one too. A whole industry was rejuvenated by the image of danger and privilege that accompanied the imported Cuban cigar.

For the next eighty years, the popularity of the cigar in America rode on the coattails of the Cuban mystique, which as time went by gained an almost occult status. Just about every top military man, every captain of industry, every famous entertainer, and every world leader smoked a big cigar, and millions imitated them.

President Calvin Coolidge was so possessive of his Havanas that when a visitor tried to wangle one by telling "Silent Cal" that his son collected cigar rings, Coolidge took the ring off one of his cherished cigars and gave it to him, leaving the cigar in the box.

Winston Churchill and his cigar forged such a close bond that the idea of England's wartime prime minister without one is unthinkable. Churchill claimed to have smoked a quarter of a million cigars in his ninety-one

Gangsters, Reel-Life and Real-Life

Edward G. Robinson was a regular customer at the Nat Sherman store in Manhattan, and so were many of the real-life "family" men of the type Robinson portrayed in the movies of the '30s and '40s. Frank Costello, Meyer Lansky, and their lieutenants would often pop in to stock up on their cigars, and so would Bugsy Siegel, whose infamous career was immortalized by the film *Bugsy,* starring Warren Beatty.

Often, my father would know these men, having grown up with them on New York's Lower East Side. I was just a kid behind the counter, and when someone from the old neighborhood would walk in, my father would give me a small, almost imperceptible wink, meaning that I should offer his childhood friend a little extra courtesy. What did Bugsy Siegel smoke? Anything he wanted to!

Al Capone. The popularity of the Havana cigar swept America in the 1930s with the advent of the gangster, who smoked Cuba's top of the line.

years. (If you do the math, that's eight and a half per day for eighty years!) During the Nazi blitz of London in 1941, one of the Luftwaffe's raids destroyed the Dunhill tobacco shop on Drake Street, in which was stored a portion of the prime minister's treasured cache of Havanas. Called to the scene in the wee hours of the morning, the store manager made a careful survey of the damage and rushed to the phone to report, "Your cigars are safe, sir."

Winston Churchill claimed to have smoked 250,000 cigars. He died at age 91.

Political leaders in my hometown of New York were serious about what they smoked, too. I recall that some of them even tried to win a few votes by being photographed in a statesmanlike pose–with a cigar clenched tenaciously between their lips. President Theodore Roosevelt and Governor Al Smith come to mind. I personally waited on many New York mayors at my father's store, starting with Fiorello LaGuardia, who read the comics to schoolchildren over the radio during a newspaper strike. New Yorkers returned the warm gesture by naming an airport after him.

"I thought I was taller" The late 1940s and early 1950s were glamorous times in New York City, and the cigar was a symbol of high living and celebrity. Sammy Davis Jr., John Wayne, and Ava Gardner were among the luminaries who would stop into the Nat Sherman shop, which was then located at 1400 Broadway, and Milton Berle, who's been a good friend and a long-time customer, had a regular routine. Milton would stand in the store, puffing away on a cigar as an admiring crowd gathered to say hello to "Mr. Television." He would then gracefully remove the cigar from his mouth, acknowledge his fans, then return the cigar to his mouth—and miss, sticking it in his nose. "I thought I was taller," he'd say. He always got a big laugh. And just try to imagine Groucho Marx without a cigar—though he never lit one in any of his many movies—or George Burns, who, by the way, smoked some of the cheapest mass-produced cigars on the market. But who cares? He loved them!

The allure of the Cuban product was fed by an army of traveling salesmen out of New York who took to the rails to spread the word throughout the country. Dapper in spats, pin-striped three-piece suits, and bowler hats, with gold watches in their pockets and lodge pins on their lapels, they worked purely on com-mission—and sold enough cigars to keep the industry humming through Depression, war, and recession.

Groucho Marx. Ever notice Groucho never lit his cigar in any of his movies?

Rat Pack Remembered

The star who attracted the biggest crowd at the Nat Sherman store had to be Sammy Davis Jr. The first day he walked in with his body-guards, there must have been fifty to a hundred people trailing him, wanting to shake his hand and asking him for his autograph. This was in his heyday, in the 1950s. There were so many fans I was afraid

they'd level the store! Sammy, who was a little man, had to come behind the counter just to protect himself from the crush.

Finally, I cleared the store and shut and locked the front doors, and still the crowds wouldn't leave. It wasn't a hostile crowd, just frightening, and I realized that this diminutive man, who was so gracious and generous, had to face this all the time. I took Sammy to my office in the back of the store, and once we were there, he asked me question after question about tobacco and cigars and where certain products were from and what he should expect from a particular brand, and so on. Despite his fame and the obvious demands it put on him—not to mention the physical peril—there was no arrogance about him whatso-

Sammy Davis Jr. Sammy was a regular Nat Sherman customer and preferred Nat Sherman No. 880 Cuban leaf cigars.

ever. He was humble and good-humored, but above all, he was curious. I admired him because he used his unique position as a celebrity as a tool to become more knowledgeable. And he apparently never forgot that day either—he was always a loyal customer. He left that day with a box of Sherman's #880 Cuban Leaf Cigar—an unusually large cigar for such a small man. I remember that as his favorite brand.

In 1954, a German refugee named Walter Frankenburg made it possible to machine-manufacture a very low-priced cigar when he invented the "homogenized" binder. This new substance was made by taking tobacco scraps and dust left over from the manufacture of higher-priced cigars (previously considered waste), blending and mixing it with a small amount of vegetable paste into a slurry, then forming it into continuous strips or paperlike sheets that were then rolled into cigars. It's less fragile and easier to handle than whole leaf and provides a uniform taste, burn, and smoothness. The practice is widespread to this day in the manufacture of less expensive cigars.

Yet, except for the occasional innovation like the homogenized binder, the American cigar industry in the first three-quarters of the twentieth century showed little imagination. Cigar makers and marketers were generally content to sell the Cuban cigar and its imitations without working to improve or refine the product–until Fidel Castro.

Embargo and innovation

Nobody in the cigar industry foresaw the catastrophic events that would follow in the wake of Castro's Communist takeover of Cuba in 1961. Everybody figured the tobacco would keep flowing and it would be business as usual. The only one who knew differently at the time was President John F. Kennedy–like most presidents, a dedicated cigar buff. Privy, obviously, to inside information, JFK laid in 1,100 Cuban-made H. Upmann Petit Coronas for the White House just before he slapped an embargo on Cuban products in June 1963.

JFK laid in 1,100 Cuban cigars for the White House just before he slapped the trade embargo on Cuba.

Nobody would have guessed at the time that the embargo would last more than thirty years.

Another thing that nobody would have guessed at the time was that Castro's ascendancy would have an inadvertent but undeniably positive effect on the development of the cigar.

One of those caught in the changing tide of Cuban politics was Ramón Cifuentes, a close friend of mine whose family originated the Partagas brand. A Spanish gentleman of the old school, he's so elegant–even at the advanced age of around ninety–that if you spent fifteen years auditioning actors to play Ramón, you'd come to the unavoidable conclusion that the only person who could do justice to his character is Ramón himself. When Castro took power, guerrillas came to confiscate Ramón's tobacco plantation and order him to leave the country. He went to his desk to get his glasses, and they told him no, you take nothing. His wife, Thalia, as charming a lady as there ever was, sneaked the family roadster out to the country and buried the family silver in the ground, where it remains to this day. Ramón and Thalia escaped to New York, where, until they could recoup some of the property they owned in Spain, they reluctantly accepted a loan from my father for living expenses.

At this time many Cuban legends in the industry moved their operations to the Canary Islands and started over from scratch, trying to grow Cuban tobacco. Ramón did not. Unfortunately for those who did move, they enjoyed limited success. That entire generation of Cuban cigar manufacturers wouldn't change their style to adapt to different growing conditions, and it wasn't until they moved back to the Caribbean in the late 1960s that the product began to show signs of improvement. Aided by a new generation that was schooled at U.S. agricultural universities like Texas A&M, manufacturers began to cross-breed, hybridize, and adapt their growing techniques to their new farms in Jamaica, the Dominican Republic, Honduras, and Mexico. The marriage of their age-old expertise, the Cuban tobacco seed with which they started, and their children's modern knowledge of agronomy, horticulture, and climatization has spawned the most creative and fruitful era of cigar making in history.

His Own "Weightlessness" in Cigars

Despite the trade embargo with Cuba, astronaut John Glenn received a gift of his weight in Havana cigars as a reward for his singular accomplishment.

John Glenn. The first American to orbit the earth later became a senator from Ohio.

Partagas Redux

When Ramón Cifuentes fled Cuba following Castro's takeover, he took his "Partagas" cigar brand with him and eventually began to make Partagas cigars in the Dominican Republic. But when the Communists confiscated the Cifuentes factory in Cuba, they, too, continued to make cigars under the Partagas name. In 1975, a U.S. court ruled that Ramón and other Cuban expatriate cigar makers have legal claim to their Cuban brand names in the United States, and many so-called "exile brands" began to spring up around the U.S. However, Cuban brands still remained throughout the rest of the world with their original frontmarks. Thus, confusion reigns as labels like Cohiba, H. Upmann, Montecristo, Por Larrañaga, Ramón Allones, Romeo y Julieta, *and* Partagas produce Cuban cigars for the rest of the world and Dominican cigars for the U.S.; and Hoyo de Monterrey, El Rey del Mundo, and Punch are made in both Cuba and Honduras. It remains to be seen if that international brand confusion will be imported into the United States when the trade embargo with Cuba is finally lifted.

Another watershed in the history of American cigar smoking was the surgeon general's landmark 1964 report on cigarette smoking. For the first time, cigarette use was allegedly linked to cancer, and cigar sales—mostly of the smaller, less expensive machine-made variety, like Tiparillo and White Owl—soared to an all-time high of nine billion.

Though the number of cigars sold in this country declined to 2 billion in 1992, consumption rose to 2.33 billion in 1994, and Americans were more discriminating and spent more money on their cigars—163 million premium cigars were sold in 1995, up from 97 million in 1991. The superior Caribbean product has rekindled interest in the entire cigar industry, and that interest has been sparked in smokers who are in their twenties and thirties, promising a robust market into the future. Analysts expect an annual 35-percent growth in sales through the 1990s. Some four hundred fifty brands are currently available in the United States, offering more than three thousand different varieties of cigar. Growers are rushing to market in order to keep up with the demand, and manufacturers are looking at back orders for the first time in years.

Celebrity Smokers

It used to be that folks found a cigar they liked and stuck with it for the rest of their lives, come hell or high water. They were loyal to a size and a brand, and that's what they smoked for twenty years.

Nowadays, however, folks like to experiment, vary their routines, try new things. I think that's great—I do it myself. So when people ask me what brand of cigar a certain celebrity smokes, I have to tell them that it varies. The brand they smoke on Sunday may not be the same one they puff on Thursday.

When I was young and worked behind the counter of my father's Manhattan smoke shop, I grew accustomed to waiting on noteworthy people. And since cigars and celebrities go together like bread and butter, many celebrities still stop in at our Fifth Avenue store to purchase their smokes. Over the years, here's what some of the stars have preferred:

George Burns: El Producto

Groucho Marx: Dunhill 410

David Letterman: Nat Sherman Dakota

Milton Berle: Nat Sherman Oxford 5

John Wayne: Nat Sherman 880

Bill Clinton: Nat Sherman Trafalgar 4

Best cigars ever

It is once again "de rigueur" to smoke cigars. Thick, glossy magazines cater to the upscale new smoker, and more and more restaurants and bars are relaxing their restrictions on cigar smoking. Celebrities like David Letterman, Sylvester Stallone, Harry Connick Jr., and Arnold Schwarzenegger keep a stash of their favorite brands at our Nat Sherman store on Manhattan's Fifth Avenue, and increasing numbers of women are enjoying a good smoke, leading to the establishment of women-only clubs like the George Sand Smoking Society, based in Santa Monica, California. Every day now, cigar smoking brings together people from disparate occupations and backgrounds and bridges gaps of age, geography, and political affiliation. Cigars

Bill Cosby: Nat Sherman Dakota

Raul Julia: Nat Sherman Hampshire

Gregory Hines: Nat Sherman Dispatch

Will Smith: Nat Sherman Gazette

Jim Belushi: Partagas No. 10

Sylvester Stallone: Nat Sherman Canary Islands No. 5

Rush Limbaugh: Nat Sherman Dakota

Woody Harrelson: Nat Sherman Butterfield 8

Harry Connick, Jr.: Nat Sherman Gramercy & Butterfield 8

Orson Wells: Macanudo No. 11

Tom Selleck: Nat Sherman Oxford No. 5

John Grisham: Nat Sherman Hampshire

Edward G. Robinson: Partagas No. 1

Charles Barkley: Nat Sherman Tribune

Robert De Niro: Nat Sherman Telegraph

Arnold Schwarzenneger: Nat Sherman Dakota

Louis Gossett, Jr.: Nat Sherman Tribeca

Whoopi Goldberg: Nat Sherman Hudson

Ernie Grunfeld: Nat Sherman Butterfield No. 8

may be the one thing President Bill Clinton and radio commentator Rush Limbaugh can agree on—though the president has to find a spot in the White House to smoke where his wife won't catch him.

Millions are catching on to one of life's greatest and most ancient of pleasures, and it is my firm belief that this recent boom has been fueled by a better product. The cigar you hold in your hand today is indeed a bit of history—the result of hundreds of years of refinement, experimentation, and sacrifice—and is undoubtedly one of the best cigars the world has ever known.

Cigars may be the one thing Bill Clinton and Rush Limbaugh can agree on.

Chapter Two

Tobacco's Journey: From Seedling to Cigar

Generations of refinement have produced the quality cigars that populate today's crowded and diverse marketplace. Improvements in tobacco breeding, curing, and blending, and in cigar manufacturing, have yielded the smoothest, most flavorful product in history—

and there's more variety, too. We owe that assortment and that high level of quality to the unceasing efforts of dozens of tobacco-growing families around the world who've carefully passed down the hallowed oral tradition from generation to generation.

And yet, essentially, today's cigars are virtually unchanged in many important ways from the first cigars that were ever smoked. The premium brands on the market are still handmade by highly trained craftspeople, in much the same way the Mayans must have done it in antiquity. It's a long and fascinating process—really an art—raising the fragile *Nicotiana tabacum* from seedling to harvest, curing it and caring for it and rolling it up into cigars that yield the wide range of flavor the best tobacco in the world is famous for. And make no mistake about it, the best tobacco goes into the making of cigars. Of all the tobacco being raised in the world today, the great majority is for cigarettes; by comparison, the amount grown for cigars is minuscule. But that small percentage of the world's tobacco harvest demands a much more vast amount of care. While cigarette tobacco is ready for rolling mere weeks after it's harvested, the process from tobacco seedling to premium cigar lasts on average about three years.

I think it's important for smokers to know what goes on during that process, because the more you know about cigars, the deeper your appreciation will be. And the deeper your appreciation, the more enjoyment you'll get each time you light up.

It's amazing how much thought and toil and care goes into the creation of a single cigar. Literally dozens of people are involved in its making, dozens of people whose individual skills are invaluable to the success of the finished product. Not only are they

Nicotiana tabacum—
the tobacco plant.

concerned with the flavor and how well the smoke can be drawn, they're deeply involved with the cigar's appearance and the quality of its presentation. Cigar rolling is considered an art form, and its practitioners, called *torcedores* in Spanish, must undergo apprenticeships of up to one year before they're even allowed to lay their hands on a *chaveta*, the rounded blade the rollers use to trim the tobacco leaves. Many of them are never promoted to the more demanding job of rolling the larger cigars, for which the best rollers are paid the highest amount of money per cigar.

Perhaps your enjoyment of cigars will be heightened by following tobacco through its journey from seedling to cigar, and by taking a look inside a cigar factory in the Dominican Republic. Without a doubt, my close personal involvement in the industry for over four decades has made me appreciate each and every cigar I smoke that much more.

Cigar parts

Before we follow the fragile tobacco seedling from farm to factory, let's take a look at the cigar's constituent parts.

Like many other cultivated plants, different tobacco plants have different kinds of leaves that serve different functions within the finished cigar. Most cigars, whether they're the premium handmade brands or the inexpensive machine-made kind, share the same construction. They all have a filler, a binder, and a wrapper. It's the successful marriage of the three that makes for a good smoke. Here's a closer look at the three elements of the cigar.

■ **Filler:** The innermost layers of tobacco in the cigar, its meat, are called the filler. Most filler leaves come from the top part of the tobacco plant. Called *ligero* leaves, they are known for their robust flavor and generally need to be aged three years before they're ready to be rolled into a quality cigar. Most handmade, high-quality cigars include a mixture of filler tobaccos from different farms and different

The filler, or bunch, leaves are the innermost portion of the cigar.

regions—even different harvests—in order to provide a smooth, flavorful smoke. It's not uncommon for a cigar to boast a veritable atlas of varying leaves from, for example, the Dominican Republic, Honduras, and Mexico.

■ **Binder:** Wrapped around the filler and inside the wrapper is the cigar's binder. The binder gives the cigar structural stability and assures an even burn. Chosen for its tensile strength, the binder leaves contribute virtually no flavor to the cigar. Without them, however, the cigar would fall apart. They are the cigar's superstructure. To a good cigar maker, the aesthetics of the wrapper leaves are very important; the beauty of the binder, however, makes no difference. The quality cigar makers look for in a binder leaf is its ability to burn evenly and maintain the cigar's shape. The binder is frequently taken from the *volado* leaves of the tobacco plant, which grow nearest the ground. Some of the best binder leaf in the world is grown in Mexico.

The binder wraps around the filler and acts as the cigar's superstructure, assuring an even burn.

■ **Wrapper:** This is the outermost layer of the cigar, and the part of the cigar that gives it its color. The Cubans call this leaf the *capa*. In the finer handmade cigars, the wrapper consists of a single tobacco leaf rolled three and a half times around the filler and binder. Exceptional care is taken to choose an attractive leaf to make up the wrapper, for this is the only part of the cigar the smoker sees when the cigar is sitting in a box. Although it's just one tobacco leaf out of anywhere from the three to seven that make up the cigar, it accounts for about 80 percent of the flavor and 100 percent of the presentation quality. If you think of a cigar as the main course of a fine meal, the filler would be the meat and the wrapper would be the spices. Another food analogy would be cake—wrapper would be the icing. Good wrapper, the most prized and expensive leaf in the cigar, should be pliable, with no prominent or protruding veins to detract from its beauty or its burning quality.

The most prized leaf of the cigar is the wrapper, which accounts for 80 percent of its flavor.

Wrapper Types

From the lightest in color to the darkest, here are the types of wrappers you'll encounter in the world of cigars. Keep in mind that the wrapper provides the cigar with about 80 percent of its flavor.

■ **Double claro, or claro claro:** from a greenish color to almost blond. This naturally pale leaf is picked prematurely and dried rapidly using wood heat. Then it's fermented for nine months. It has a very light flavor. The greenish wrapper, called *candela*, was supremely popular in the United States in the 1960s

but is more rare today. Macanudo calls this color wrapper "jade." Also called "American Market Selection," or AMS.

■ **Claro:** darker than the double claro, but still very light brown. Also a naturally pale leaf, the claro is picked prematurely and then undergoes about forty-eight days of natural drying in the barn and then twelve months of fermentation. The Connecticut shade-grown wrapper is a good example of this lighter, mellower leaf with a delicate aroma.

■ **Colorado claro and colorado:** light brown color with a reddish tinge. Called "natural," "English Market Selection," or EMS, a good example would be the finer wrapper leaves now coming out of Mexico that are smooth but provide a spicy flavor as well.

Some of the best and most popular wrapper in the world is what's called "shade-grown." The tobacco is grown under giant gauze shades to protect it from the sun and keep its oiliness to a minimum. Some of the best wrapper leaf in the world is grown under shade in Connecticut. Cameroon, Sumatra, and Honduras are all well-known for growing high-quality wrapper leaf.

- **Colorado maduro and maduro:** Maduro means "ripe," or "mature," but naturally mature leaves, with their characteristic dark brown–almost black–color haven't been grown since the late 1980s because of the expense. Rather, growers steam the less delicate, more mature leaves to give them their darker color and fuller body. I like to compare the maduro leaf to a chocolate mousse–it's full-bodied, robust, and fit for what can be described as a "dessert cigar." Most of the wrapper leaf that comes out of Cameroon is fuller-bodied, too, but without the blackish color. The Cameroon

wrapper is more like a colorado maduro–a darker brown but not fully darkened. Also called "Spanish Market Selection."

- **Oscuro:** Being black, they are the darkest cigars on the market. Oscuro leaf is grown in the open field, without shade, and the leaves are picked when mature. Originally selected as the darkest of the maduro leaves, the oscuro leaf is now steamed in the same manner as the maduro. However, it's getting harder to find oscuros due to the expense of growing tobacco leaves for so long. It has a negligible aroma, but it's very full-bodied.

No book can tell you how
to grow great tobacco.

Tobacco from top to bottom

Tobacco leaves vary in quality from the top of the plant to the bottom. Here are the three basic categories of tobacco that are used inside the cigar.

- **Ligero:** The topmost leaves of the tobacco plant are called the ligero. Because of their greater exposure to the sun (except, of course, in the case of the shade-grown tobaccos), they are the darkest, oiliest, heartiest in flavor, and most defined as far as veins are concerned. These leaves generally burn fastest and the roller must take great care to bunch ligero leaves in the middle of the cigar's filler. Placed too close to the wrapper, the ligero leaves will cause the cigar to burn unevenly or too rapidly. Because of their oily, robust qualities, ligero leaves need to be aged a minimum of three years before they can be rolled into a cigar.

- **Seco:** Less spicy and lighter in color than the top ligero leaves, these leaves from the center part of the tobacco plant are valued for their beauty as well as their mild flavor. Seco leaves mature in about eighteen months.

- **Volado:** The bottom leaves on the tobacco plant, the volado leaves contain the least amount of oil of any of the leaves and hence taste the lightest. They are valued more for their burning qualities, and hence often are used as binder. They require a minimum of nine months of aging before they can be rolled into a cigar.

Ligero

Seco

Volado

Ligero, seco, and volado leaves are all part of the roller's workbench, but their proportion in the finished cigar is determined well ahead of time by the manufacturer according to the taste and burning qualities he wants from the cigar. The more robust varieties of cigars will need to have a higher proportion of ligero leaves, while some of the milder brands may not have any ligero leaves at all.

In handmade cigars, the filler is fashioned from separate leaves folded by hand along their length to allow a clear smoking passage through which the smoke can be drawn. This style of folding the filler leaves along the length of the cigar is called the "book" method, because if you cut the cigar down its length with a blade, the filler leaves resemble the pages of a book.

Methods of manufacture

Now that you know the constituent parts of a cigar and what kinds of leaves go to make the filler, the binder, and the wrapper, the next step is to visualize the different methods manufacturers use to actually put the leaves together to make a cigar. For the better part of the rest of this chapter, I'll be describing how a seedling becomes a premium-quality, handmade cigar. But keep in mind that handmade cigars are only one type of cigar available to the smoker. Though the price of a cigar certainly depends a great deal on the quality of the tobacco, it depends more on the way the cigar is put together.

Here's a list of the major ways cigar manufacturers construct their products, starting with the type of cigar that's generally more costly and working down in expense.

■ **Long-filled, handmade:** The term "long-filled" refers to the practice of using whole leaves as the filler. These are generally the highest class of cigar, since the product is carefully handmade from start to finish by the factory's most expert workers. The whole-leaf fillers are usually a mix of different types of tobacco blended to provide the best-quality smoke. Sometimes, cigar makers will blend leaves from three, four–even five–different growing areas and harvests to come up with the most satisfying filler combination.

Dozens of highly skilled people are involved in the making of a single cigar.

■ **Machine-bunched, hand-rolled:** With the scarcity and the difficulty of training meticulously skilled cigar rollers–who, especially in this highly mechanized age, are rare and prized–many manufacturers resort to a foot-operated, semiautomatic device for bunching the filler and binder of the cigars into a cylindrical shape. The wrapper is then rolled on by hand. This is a perfectly fine alternative to a completely handmade cigar, and it can bring the price of the finished product down some. Sometimes price is the only discernible difference between the two types! The quality of the tobacco can be similar or the same as the handmade cigars, as the leaves are still whole and are hand-picked.

- **Completely machine-made:** Once you've been smoking cigars for a while, you can tell a completely machine-rolled cigar from a hand-rolled cigar–the quality is that much different. A machine bunches the filler and binder and the same machine rolls a wrapper around it. Some manufacturers of smaller cigars can produce dozens of cigars a minute on fully automated rolling machines.

- **Machine-made with homogenized binder:** Homogenized–or HTL, for homogenized tobacco leaf–binder is made from tobacco leaves or the shavings from whole leaves that are pulverized, mixed with a vegetable gum made from cellulose and water, and rolled into long sheets. This substance is then cut and rolled into the cigar. The result is a binder that's stronger than a whole-leaf binder, which is essential if the cigar is to survive the somewhat harsh thrashing it can undergo in a typical mass-production facility, where hundreds of cigars can be pumped out every minute. When you see a warning on the package that reads CONTAINS NONTOBACCO PRODUCTS, that refers to the small amount of vegetable product and water that's added to the tobacco to make the homogenized binder. Ninety percent of mass-market cigars are made with homogenized binder.

- **Short-filled "bunch":** Though the quality can vary greatly, all short-filled cigars have one thing in common–their filler is made of bits and pieces of tobacco instead of whole leaves. In the case of the least expensive varieties, this is because the filler is made of the discarded tobacco from the more expensive whole-leaf-filler cigars. In other cases, it allows the manufacturer to fill the cigar with dozens of types of tobacco, improving the quality, or at least making the product more distinctive. "Bunch" is another word for filler.

■ **Homogenized wrapper:** Ever wonder why some mass-produced cigars lack leaf veins on their wrappers? That's because manufacturers wrap the cigars with homogenized tobacco. A while back, some of the mass-market companies experimented with whole-leaf wrappers, but smokers revolted. The sight of the leaf veins made them uneasy, and the makers went back to the homogenized wrapper, which provides a smooth, dull finish to the outer layer of the cigar, and no veins. The homogenized wrapper also enables manufacturers to add flavorings, like rum, cherry, or vanilla. The homogenized wrapper is indicative of the "dry" cigars originally developed by the Dutch that are so popular around the world. The cigar with the homogenized wrapper is usually short-filled—and usually among the least expensive of the cigars on the market. Sixty percent of what's referred to as mass-market cigars are made with homogenized wrapper.

From a tiny seed

All varieties of cigar tobacco start their lives as seeds that are so small that a thousand can fit inside a thimble. Yet from these tiny pinpoints of future tobacco plants, entire empires have been built! Native to Central America, tobacco is now grown on all the continents but Antarctica (though perhaps an enterprising soul is cultivating tobacco there, too). There has been so much cross-breeding and hybridization over the years—with Cameroon seed being grown in Ecuador, for instance,

A thousand tobacco seeds can fit inside a thimble.

and Connecticut seed being grown in Honduras—that a lot of the natural attributes of different cigar tobaccos in different areas of the world have been diminished or lost. This isn't necessarily a bad thing, because whenever a seed is grown far away from its origin, its process of adjustment to the different conditions can result in a superior product—or at least a different, intriguing product—as compared to the homegrown variety. Think of tobacco in the same way you'd think of wine grapes. Some wine drinkers nowadays prefer California Chardonnay to its French predecessor, just as some cigar smokers prefer Dominican blended cigars to their forerunners, the heavy Cuban varieties.

No matter where it's grown, the type of seed the farmer starts with is one-third of the equation in growing quality cigar tobacco and will determine, along with the soil and climate, the tobacco's future characteristics of color, taste, and aroma.

Those are the natural elements that determine the quality and type of tobacco—seed, soil, and climate. Even if all those conditions are perfect, there's no guarantee a tobacco crop will be a success. What's just as important as those natural variables is the wisdom and experience of the grower and his workers.

You can't teach it

An old vaudevillian used to tell the story about new parents who were trying to get their baby to stop crying. They were in the infant's bedroom, thumbing desperately through the latest how-to book on child-rearing while Grandmother, who was not allowed in the room because she wasn't sterile, watched from the doorway, biting her tongue. Finally, as the baby's shrieks reached crescendo, Grandma could contain herself no longer and offered her homespun, "uneducated" advice: "Put down the book and pick up the baby!"

Similarly, there's no book written on how to grow fine cigar tobacco. It's a plant that's so fragile and requires such careful hands-on tending that a whole crop could go bad while you're thumbing through the book, looking for answers. More than anything, it requires a special intuitive sense that can only be learned by doing. That's why so many growers come from tobacco-farming families. The expertise has been passed on from generation to generation, through experience rather than through how-to guides.

This Connecticut tobacco field is shielded from the sun by sheets of gauze, which will reduce the oiliness of the leaves and make for a mel-low—and more expensive—cigar.

The tobacco plant starts on its journey to becoming a cigar as a seedling grown in seedbeds where cigar smoking by the indoor gardeners is expressly forbidden. Cigar ashes can contain viruses that have the ability to destroy the frail seedlings. After six weeks, the hardier plants are ready for the outdoors and must be transplanted by hand, with precise distances between them. Needless to say, that makes it a very labor-intensive crop—and the work's just begun. Jobs like weeding the beds and snipping off the plant's buds—to prevent the stunting of the growth of the leaves—need to be done entirely by hand. For shade-grown tobacco, which is used for the best wrapper, entire fields need to be shadowed under giant skeins of muslin gauze, called *tapados* in Spanish, which hang ten feet off the ground over the plants to keep out the direct sunlight. They are propped up by wooden staves driven into the ground and must be attached and detached by workers on stilts.

A lot can go wrong

After six weeks of growing, the plant grows as tall as six feet. During this period, the tobacco farmer experiences heart palpitations due to the numerous things that could go awry for his tender crop. Weather hazards, for example, haunt growers of every stripe. In the case of tobacco, farmers pray against rain; dry conditions are essential for optimal yield. Tobacco plants don't even need irrigation—morning dew and an occasional light drizzle are the only watering tobacco requires. So you can imagine what hurricanes and other violent storms that plague the Caribbean can do to an entire planting—wipe it out, either quickly, with their strong winds, or slowly, with flooding. In addition to the potential for climactic horrors, the tobacco planter faces the prospect of ruination from ants, leaf borers, stem borers, root borers, crickets, spores, parasitic plants, fungi, disease, and molds of different colors. A fungus called blue mold wiped out the entire Cuban harvest of 1980 and severely hampered it again in 1995, robbing the tobacco industry there of some $100 million in revenue with each epidemic. The same sinister spore slaughtered tobacco plants in the Dominican Republic in 1984, and Honduras and Nicaragua were hit by its devastating wave the following year. Honduras is still recovering from blue mold epidemics in 1993 and 1995 that ravaged an estimated quarter of its tobacco yield.

Fortunately for the planter, some of the risks associated with pests and bad weather are mitigated by business arrangements that can be cut before the season gets under way. Typically, a cigar manufacturer will subsidize an experienced farmer for an entire field of tobacco before it's even planted. Of course, this isn't a blind decision to just give away money, it's based on years of relationships between the farmer and the manufacturer. That doesn't mean that it's not a gamble. If it's a poor growing season, the quality of the tobacco may not live up to expectations, in which case the manufacturer can keep whatever tobacco meets his standards and auction off the rest. But if it's a good growing sea-

---

Devastation row: ants, leaf borers, stem borers, root borers, crickets, spores, parasitic plants, fungi, disease, and blue and white mold.

---

son, the investment can more than pay off—for the manufacturer as well as the smoker, who will enjoy the high quality of the cigars that will be manufactured from the bumper yield.

It used to be that certain regions—like Brazil, for example—grew tobacco for a localized market, and whenever any of their cigar tobacco was exported, it was more because of expatriate demand than it was a part of any kind of marketing scheme. But with the recent surge in the popularity of cigars, consumer demand drives the quality and quantity of the worldwide supply of tobacco, and because tobacco has one of the highest cash returns per acre of any crop, most of the appropriate available farmland is being sought for the cultivation of cigar tobacco, and production has

Priming, or picking, the tobacco is an extremely labor-intensive task. Workers must be very careful not to damage the fragile leaves.

become very sensitive to the demands of the marketplace. Mexican farmers, for instance, who once grew only binder and low-grade filler tobacco, are now beginning to produce the higher-quality product that will result in better sales in the United States.

About forty-five days after transplanting, it's time for priming, or harvesting, which must be done by hand so as not to harm the plant or its delicate leaves. This is a painstaking process. The pickers roll out a canvas carpet and drop the picked leaves on it. On each pass through the field, the pickers take the leaves off a particular section of the plants. Generally, there are six primings, one for each level of the plant, starting at the bottom of the plant, where the leaves mature the fastest, and working up to the top. When they're done snipping the leaves off the plant, the workers roll up the canvas. This method assures that the delicate leaves won't be damaged.

Nothing is wasted in the process; all the leaves are used. It used to be that the lowest leaves on the tobacco plant were dropped into the soil to make fertilizer, but today it's just not cost-effective to do that. The lowest leaves are now used as filler for lower-priced cigars.

From farm to barn

From the field, the green tobacco leaves are carried to the curing barns, where they are sewn together into bundles of about fifteen to fifty called "hands" and left to hang. Hundreds and hundreds of tobacco leaves hang from the rafters of these curing barns, their chlorophyll draining out of them, until about six weeks have passed and their green color has been replaced by brown and their smooth texture has transformed into a crinkly, somewhat withered appearance.

Though the tobacco crop brings a very lucrative return per acre for the grower, one of the drawbacks of growing tobacco is that each field must be kept fallow one year out of every three in order for the proper level of

A tobacco field needs to lie fallow one year in three.

nutrients to be maintained in the soil. Part of the problem with the post-Castro crops of Cuban tobacco is the state farmers' reluctance to leave fields fallow as much as they ought to. Without fertilizer, pesticides, and the right amount of nutrition in the soil, the tobacco crops there have suffered. Also, tobacco farmers must grow a certain amount of tobacco each season for seed. That means that about one-third of a farm's acreage in any given year is not producing tobacco for harvest. You can see why the Cubans are tempted to take shortcuts—the short-term yield is so much better if you don't take the necessary steps to ensure long-term productivity.

In Connecticut, the growing season is, of course, shorter than in the Caribbean and lasts long enough for just one harvest. In the Caribbean, Mexico, and Central America, where most of the world's cigar tobacco is grown, two harvests can be eked out in the course of a calendar year.

A delicate balance

The curing barns are where the growers must have a real nose for their tobacco or they can lose the value of their entire crop. Tobacco must be checked every four hours all day and all night, seven days a week, while it's curing. Otherwise an entire barnful can turn sour in a matter of hours, and the value of leaves that usually fetch up to forty dollars a pound can plummet to about four dollars a pound. The reason: Slight but lethal variations in temperature and humidity can wreck the drying leaves. Since the tobacco has to be aged at just the right speed, farmers use slats in the side of the barn to regulate drying temperature, a procedure called "venting."

After their six-week stay in the curing barns, the leaves are carefully removed, sorted by color, and divided into stacks. These stacks are hauled into rooms where they will be left to ferment or, in the trade parlance, to sweat. Workers measure the temperature inside the stacks of the fermenting leaves and rotate the leaves from the inside of the stacks to the outside,

(*Above, left*) **Movable staves help regulate the temperature inside this Connecticut curing barn.**

(*Above, right*) **A cured tobacco leaf is brown because its chlorophyll has been replaced by carotene.**

(*Right*) **Workers at a Dominican Republic cigar factory sort leaves by color.**

never letting the temperature of the leaves remain above 112 degrees Fahrenheit for too long. During this fermentation process, ammonia is released by the leaves, and the fermentation rooms are so full of its over-powering aroma that your eyes water when you enter them. I give those workers a lot of credit for being able to withstand that kind of stinging.

From the fermentation rooms, workers again sort the leaves according to color, texture, and size. Some leaves are designated for filler, some for binder, and the best for wrapper. You'd be surprised how often the tobacco leaves are sorted by highly trained workers. Each leaf can go through as many as a dozen selection processes, all designed to sort the leaves perfectly. Broken leaves are rejected for any purpose but filler. All leaves at this point have their main vein/stem removed. This is called the stripping process.

In order to assure an even burn, veins are removed from some of the leaves.

The tobacco leaves are then wrapped tightly in bales and kept in storehouses, which allow them to ferment at a constant humidity for another, longer period of time–sometimes up to two years.

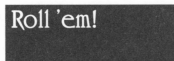

Roll 'em!

Once the tobacco leaves have been fermented to the point where their flavors have stabilized, it's time for skilled workers to roll them into the premium handmade cigars that are enjoyed by cigar enthusiasts throughout the world. Most of the time this means that the tobacco will be transported from the farm's barns to the factories where the cigars are actually rolled. Sometimes this merely means crossing a dirt road; most of the time it means a trip on a cargo ship or transport plane.

Cigar factories in the Dominican Republic are an endless source of fascination to me. They are usually either small, primitively built mom-and-pop operations or the more substantial–and more common–concrete buildings that reside in the island nation's duty-free zones, where the tobacco is imported and rolled and the finished cigars are loaded onto trucks to be taken to the airport, all within a small geographic area. The smaller operations employ the whole family. Usually mom and the children are skilled rollers, dad takes care of business, and tidiness is secondary. The larger factories have the same feel, only they're bigger and the employees aren't all related. But the one thing that truly links them all is the overwhelming feeling that the workers are deeply connected to the product, to the land on which it is grown, and to the industry that provides them with a livelihood. This feeling connects my family in the United States to theirs in the Dominican Republic, and makes us all part of a common enterprise. It's almost as if the convivial atmosphere generated by cigar smoking is begun while the cigars are in their infancy, at the work tables of the cigar rollers themselves.

Once at the rolling factory, the leaves, which have dried out somewhat and aged in bales in transport, must be steamed to get their moisture level back up to standard. Once they're rehydrated, they're sorted yet again, and the ones destined to become filler, binder, and wrapper are deposited on the wooden work tables used by the *torcedores* to work their magic upon.

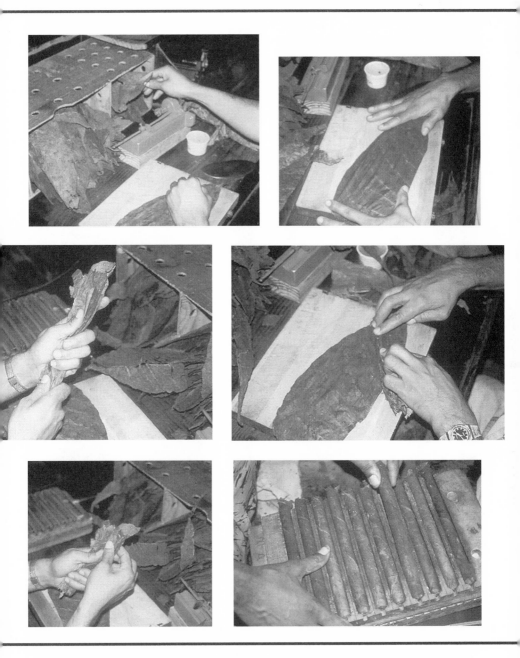

A *torcedor* in a Dominican factory selects leaves for his filler and rolls them into a bunch. Then he wraps the filler in a binder leaf and places the bunch in a cylindrical mold, to hold it together in the shaper until the wrapper leaf can be applied.

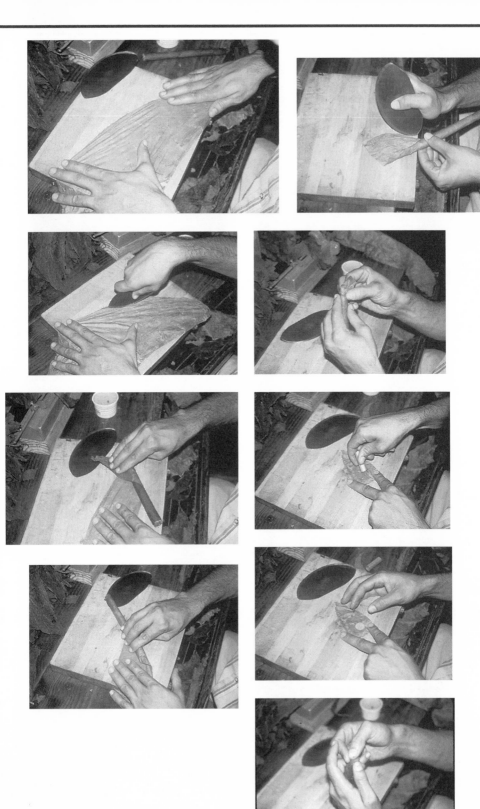

Rolling the wrapper leaf requires extensive training and skill and an intuitive feel for the cigar. First, the *torcedor* stretches the leaf a bit, then places the bunch of filler and binder leaves on top of it. After rolling the wrapper leaf three and a half times around the bunch, the *torcedor* trims it with his *chaveta*. The cap is then fashioned out of a circle cut from a tobacco leaf and carefully fitted on the crown of the cigar. These photos were taken in a Dominican factory that makes Nat Sherman cigars.

Some of these work tables have cubbyholes where the different leaves are sorted for easy retrieval.

Depending on the size of the cigar to be rolled, anywhere from two to six leaves are used for the filler. They are usually a blend of different varieties of tobacco, from different plantations in different regions. A big part of the fun of being involved in the development of different cigar types over the years for me has been the mixing and matching of the varieties of leaves. I feel like a vintner who blends different grapes to get just the right taste in his wine, or the scotch maker who blends different whiskies. So much of it is personal taste and figuring what kinds of blends you can deliver to the smoker consistently over a period of time.

The filler leaves are bunched and a binder leaf is rolled around it to keep it all together. Great skill is required to distribute the filler leaves in just the right manner so the finished cigar will produce the right draw— too little and the cigar will be "plugged," meaning the smoker will get red in the face sucking on it; too much and the smoker will be blasted with smoke and the cigar will burn unevenly. The unfinished cigars are then squeezed into wooden molds, awaiting the wrapper.

Now comes the tricky part. With a rounded blade something like half a pizza cutter called a *chaveta,* the expert roller trims off any extra tobacco from the filler and begins to roll. The wrapper goes around the filler and binder three and a half times and is secured with a few drops of vegetable paste to make it stick together.

Next, a piece of the wrapper about the circumference of a quarter is cut out of a leaf of wrapper tobacco to fashion the crown of the cigar. Sometimes the *torcedor* will actually use a coin to trace out the tobacco for cutting. It's curved, then attached to the end of the cigar to close it.

The finished cigar is then put through a rigorous series of tests to determine that it is the exact length and thickness, called "ring gauge," it is supposed to be, then the ring is put on (see Chapter Three). After that, the cigars are sorted by color to ensure as little variation as possible and loaded by hand into boxes.

The quality of the cigars is checked, rechecked, and checked again. The cigars must all have proper length, girth, and draw before they're sorted by wrapper color. You'd be surprised what minute variations in wrapper color these Dominican workers can detect with the naked eye.

The stuff of magic

When I was a child, cigar boxes were a magical thing to me. I remember they were handmade from cedar and meticulously assembled–sturdy, but always lighter than they looked, light enough for me to carry. The cedar gave off an intoxicating fragrance from ten paces, and when I opened a box and stuck my nose inside, I breathed deeply of what remained of the aroma of tobacco, and it smelled exotic and exciting and adult. In the plain wood boxes I put my crayons, or baseball cards, or coins. But the cigar boxes dressed up in fancy labels and decorated with scenes of the tranquil Caribbean–long-gowned Spanish maidens carrying bunches of red roses in woven baskets beneath the palms, or waterside Indians in loincloths and headdresses hailing bearded Europeans in their colorful sloops–these boxes I saved for my games of imagination. The cigar box belonged to Pandora, it was home to Aladdin's genie, it was the ticking heart from Edgar Allan Poe. I cherished the romance all the more because the boxes were gifts from my father.

Even with a dad in the tobacco business, my first encounter with cigars was through the boxes he brought home for me. And maybe that's part of the romance for me today, the cigar boxes I remember so

The Ring Test

My old friend Ramón Cifuentes, whose family originated the Partagas brand in Cuba–and who still, in his nineties, oversees the expatriate Partagas operation in the Dominican Republic– had the most rigorous test for his rollers I've ever seen employed. On the third finger of his right hand, he wore a ring that was the exact diameter of the Partagas No. 1, ring gauge 43. On his periodic and very grand tours of his rolling facility, he would slip the ring off his finger and slip it on a newly rolled Partagas No. 1. If the ring slid on snugly but without too much resistance, the roller was given the thumbs-up. If Ramón had trouble fitting the ring on the cigar, or if the ring hung too loosely from the cigar, woe be unto the roller. Ramón would spare his life but often not his job.

fondly from childhood. I had the opportunity to give them to my own children, and they, someday, will give cigar boxes to theirs.

Very little has changed about cigar boxes since they were first used in the 1830s. Back then, Herman Upmann was a London banker just dabbling in cigar production, and when he commissioned his Cuban factory to send samples back to his banker buddies in England, they were packed in cedar boxes. I don't know if the tradition of using cedar goes back before then or if cedar was simply the most available material at the time, but when Mr. Upmann took the plunge and went exclusively into the cigar trade, they recognized the obvious advantages of the redolent wood and made the practice famous. Even today, most

A Macanudo "wrap set" or "dress box."

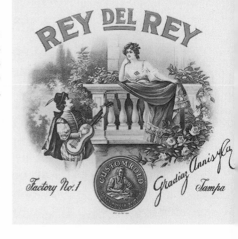

Detail from a Rey del Rey (King of Kings) "dress box" design. Such romantic scenes are typical of cigar-box labels. The Annis family, makers of Rey del Rey, was a top Tampa cigar maker for decades.

Caribbean cigar makers use African cedar grown in Honduras, and not only for boxes. Cigar tube liners are usually made of paper-thin sheets of cedar, too.

What the Cubans knew back in 1830 is still true today—there's something about the relationship between cedar and tobacco that's made in heaven. They not only augment and complement each other's aromas, but cedar also keeps the cigar from drying out. There's no sensation that quite rivals the feeling when you open a new box of cigars and breathe in that blend of cedar and tobacco for the first time.

Other aspects of the cigar box remain the same today as when I was a kid. They're still handmade and there are still two kinds. The cabinet box is the name for the plain-wood kind, flat with brass hinges that won't rust in the humidor. They sometimes come equipped with fancy clasps, called broaches, that add a touch of class. The other is the one I used to imagine was magical. It's called the "dress box," or "wrap set," and it's still covered in a label that trumpets the brand name, with lush scenes of the tranquil Caribbean. Of course, now they're magical to me more because of the cigars with which they're filled.

Today, we use a variety of special boxes. Leather binding, slide-off tops, rounded corners, vertical packaging—even glass jars—are all popular. These are pricier, but they're also charming, reusable, and make a terrific impression when given as gifts.

I love this desktop leather humidor, hand-tooled in 24-karat gold. It's called the Katahdin and can preserve up to 50 cigars.

Rounded corners, vertical packaging, and a sliding lid all make for unique, eye-catching cigar boxes.

Finishing touches

Some cigar makers add a little finishing touch to make their products distinctive. A ribbon, a square of tissue paper, metal tubes with cedar linings—all are intended to set their cigar apart from the others, to make you want to buy it and be proud to spend your hard-earned money on it. Some cigar boxes nowadays even feature the names of the factory workers responsible for choosing the cigars that went into it. I think that's a fine thing—a link between you, the smoker, and the many people who work so diligently to bring you a high-quality product, partners in the making and enjoyment of a world-class cigar.

Tobacco around the world

Each tobacco-growing region in the world offers a unique set of circumstances that influence the quality and availability of its tobacco crop. The possible length of growing seasons, climate, availability of knowledgeable and skilled workers, agreeable soil—even political conditions—all contribute to the success or failure of the product.

Generally speaking, soil that's on the sandy side, a balmy climate, and a long tradition of tobacco-raising make the best bets for cigar tobacco, but all those qualities exist in Cuba, for instance, and Cuban cigars—for purely political reasons—are unavailable in the United States. Similarly, copacetic climate, the proper soil, and favorable political conditions exist elsewhere in the world—like Ecuador—yet the tobacco of that country hasn't made much of a dent in the world market because the know-how lags behind the natural conditions—so far. Keep in mind that it takes four to five years for a tobacco crop to come to market in the form of cigars, so that in a relatively short period of time certain regions may be able to reverse their lukewarm reputations and start producing a top-notch cigar. Mexico, for one, was home to a tobacco crop that a few short years ago was considered worthy only as binder for premium cigars. Today, it produces fine wrapper and filler tobacco. Yet many so-called cigar experts still look down on Mexican cigar tobacco because of its now-outdated reputation.

Just as each region grows tobacco with particular characteristics that set it apart from the rest of the industry, so are various areas home to different factories that produce cigars with varying reputations. But the fact of the matter is, most cigars on the market today are there because people like to smoke them. Otherwise, the brands would have disappeared without a trace long ago! This may seem like an obvious point, but I like to bring it up to counteract the snobbery that exists among some cigar enthusiasts today.

Here's a look at the different tobacco-growing and cigar-making regions of the world.

■ **Cuba:** Once the only place in the world where premium cigars were made, Cuba was the origin of much of the cigar mystique. But since the United States clamped a trade embargo on the Caribbean-island nation in 1963, the high quality of the cigars of other countries, like the Dominican Republic and Honduras, has equalled the Cuban product.

Cuba has four major growing regions. From east to west, they are: Oriente, Remedios, Partido (near Havana), and the most famous, the Vuelta Abajo, located in the island's westernmost province of Pinar del Rio.

The balmy climate and sandy soil of Cuba offer good conditions for growing cigar tobacco. The average temperature on the island is 75 degrees Fahrenheit, and the average humidity is 80 percent. About 100,000 undulating acres of Vuelta Abajo's reddish, sandy soil is planted with tobacco, and by law farmers are required to sell their produce to the state. Since the

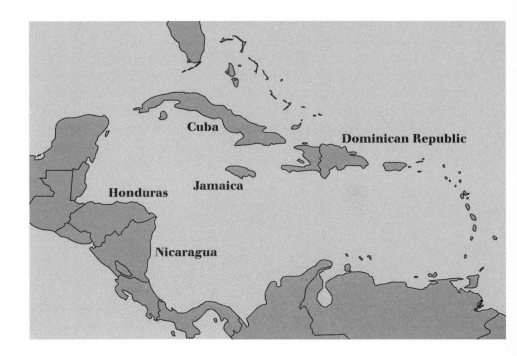

Castro revolution, they've each been allowed to own only 150 acres privately.

Cuba's growing season extends from November to February, the driest time of the year. The Partido area yields a top-notch leaf, while less expensive cigars are made in the Remedios and Oriente regions. Some fine wrapper, binder, and filler tobaccos are harvested in Pinar del Rio, though very little of it finds its way to the United States–none of it legally. It's estimated that about five million Cuban cigars are smoked within the United States in a given year. Because the vast majority of them are smuggled in, it's impossible to know the number for sure.

Though the island's traditional largest trading partner–the United States –hasn't imported its most renowned product since the trade embargo, Cuba currently has eight factories producing cigars for the rest of the worldwide market. That's down from an all-time high of 120 factories in the first decade of the twentieth century.

Tobacco remains Cuba's fourth-biggest export, after sugar, nickel, and fruit. But the rest of the world would be hard-pressed to match the Cubans cigar for cigar. Cuba's population of fourteen million people consumes three hundred million cigars a year! Compare that to the estimated sixty million cigars the island exported in 1995.

Growing conditions have suffered in recent years, and the Cuban government, which until recently exercised a monopoly over the cigar industry, has fallen on hard times in the wake of the Soviet Union's dissolution. Not only is there a dearth of working capital–six billion dollars a year came from the Soviets–but there's a constant shortage of fertilizers and pesticides. Hurricane Andrew cut a devastating swath through Cuban tobacco crops in 1993, and the industry is just now catching up.

In 1994, a private company, Habanos S.A., replaced the state-owned Cubatabaco as Cuba's monopoly cigar maker and immediately came up with a capitalist-inspired plan to finance future tobacco crops–the customers, most of them European countries like Spain, France, Britain, and Switzerland and Middle Eastern countries like Saudi Arabia, were to pay for their cigars before the tobacco was even planted. Manufacturers from the United States have been doing this for years in countries like Honduras and the Dominican Republic. With the new administration of the Cuban cigar industry, goals are being set higher, too. Habanos S.A. hopes to sell ninety million Havanas worldwide by the end of the century.

Though Castro himself quit smoking some years ago, he still dispenses his Cohiba brand to visiting dignitaries. Cohiba, named for the pre-Columbian Taino Indian word for tobacco, was developed in 1961 by Castro's first minister of industry–a man who's famous in his own right, Che Guevara–as the preeminent showcase Cuban cigar. Also part of the reason for its establishment was the legal limbo many of the famous Cuban brands faced in the wake of the trade embargo. Because the proprietorship of those brand names was–and still remains–a mystery, Castro figured he needed a brand of his own just in case the others were awarded to Cuban exiles. When it came to marketing cigars, even the Communist revolutionaries knew the benefits of a slick campaign. Cohibas are made from tobacco grown only in the ten best vegas, or plantations, in the Vuelta Abajo region, and the leaves are aged through an additional, third fermentation period. Only women roll the Cohiba cigars. The brand's costliness reflects these refinements; it's the most expensive brand to come out of Cuba, and possibly the most sought-after cigar in all the world.

Along with Cohiba, Cuba is home to some of the oldest cigar brands in the world, like Por Larrañaga (established 1834, it's the oldest Cuban brand still in production), H. Upmann (founded in 1844 by the banker Herman Upmann), Hoyo de Monterrey (introduced in 1867 by José Gener, whose name still adorns the cigar bands), El Rey del Mundo (1848), Partagas

(1845), Ramón Allones (1839), Romeo y Julieta (1875), and famous brands like Montecristo and Fonseca. As I've mentioned before, cigars bearing many of these Cuban brand names are also manufactured elsewhere in the Caribbean or in Honduras, making the same cigar available to American smokers despite the trade embargo which has proscribed the importation of the Cuban counterparts.

Though the mystique of the Cuban cigar powered the U.S. cigar industry as a whole for most of the twentieth century, and many cigar enthusiasts still genuflect when they hear the name "Cuba," I maintain that the cigars coming out of Honduras, Mexico, and the Dominican Republic today are superior to the Cuban. Premium cigars—the product Cuba made famous—are more popular today than ever before, and the reason is that the product is simply better. It's more refined, it's mellower, it's smoother, it's more sophisticated. The Cubans have always been well-known for rushing their product to market, so most Cuban cigars aren't cured long enough; when you take a puff, you feel a burning sensation in your chest—testimony to the high ammonia content of the cigars, due to lack of proper aging. Back in the 1950s, like a lot of smokers, I clenched my teeth and grinned through the experience of smoking a Havana. They were such a famous product, they had to be good, right? But when all was said and done, it took an almost macho disregard for discomfort to smoke one all the way down, and I never looked forward to the next one.

Despite the fact that a smoother, less overpowering type of cigar has begun to dominate the U.S. market, many of America's smokers today—too young to have ever smoked a legal Havana—remain enamored of the Cuban cigar. Or rather, they remain enamored of the Cuban mystique. By all means, try one if you're traveling in another country. But don't be surprised if it's not everything you dreamed it would be!

■ **Dominican Republic:** Thanks to the Communist takeover of Cuba and the subsequent U.S. trade embargo against Cuban cigars, the Dominican Republic has become the world's leader in the manufacture of premium-quality cigars, accounting for nearly half the handmade cigar sales in the United States—sixty-seven million in 1994 alone. The brands that emanate from the Dominican Republic are a Who's Who of the cream of the premium-cigar trade. The rich, dark topsoil of this small Caribbean nation—which shares an island with the politically chaotic country of Haiti—has proved to be a deservedly lauded successor to Cuba. Aiding in the Dominican Republic's meteoric rise to the top rank of the cigar-making world has been the presence of a number of Cuban expatriates—

like Ramón Cifuentes, hounded out of their native land by Castro–who, after a brief and largely fruitless stint in the Canary Islands, settled in the Dominican Republic and pretty much duplicated their earlier success.

It wasn't until about 1980 that the Dominican cigar business really got moving. Once the Cuban expatriates planted their Cuban seed, it thrived in the mineral-rich soils and balmy climate, which are similar to Cuba's. Ironically, the two fertile Dominican valleys–the Real Valley and the Cibao River Valley–yield only filler and binder tobacco. Though these tobaccos stand among the world's best, the soil and climactic conditions of the Dominican Republic have yet to produce as high-quality a wrapper leaf. Dominican cigar makers must therefore import wrapper leaf, and a majority of it comes from places like Connecticut (for a lighter smoke) and Cameroon (for the fuller-bodied).

Though many connoisseurs say that the Cuban cigar has never been duplicated outside of Cuba, I think the Dominican product is clearly better. I prefer its smoother, less overpowering quality. Dominican-made cigars are a pleasure we owe to Fidel Castro!

■ **Honduras:** When the world's most celebrated cigar makers were forced to flee Cuba, they looked far and wide for a place that offered similar growing conditions–sympathetic climate, rich soil–to their native island's. Many of them retained dual citizenship in Spain, so they avoided immigration hassles by settling in the Canary Islands; others returned to the Caribbean in the 1970s and established farms and factories in the Dominican Republic and Jamaica.

An enterprising few trekked to the remote Jalapa Valley of Honduras and found the soil so singularly sweet and the conditions so amenable to the raising of cigar tobacco that no obstacle seemed too great to prevent them from reestablishing their tobacco farms and realizing their dream. The steep, rugged mountains that surround the Jalapa Valley had to be tamed. Roads were built and farms were fashioned from scratch. Because of the elevation and the harsh terrain, custom vehicles had to be ordered, with four-wheel-drive transmissions and special high-altitude carburetors. Though commercial tobacco farms in Honduras date from the eighteenth century and Cuban seed was said to be introduced there in 1941, it wasn't until the early 1970s that the small, poor, Central American country began to make its mark on the world scene. A world-class leaf began to be exported, one that some enthusiasts say is closest in quality to the Cuban, and with refinement, the product has gotten even better. The land of the Mayans–those original cigar smokers–is now the world's second-leading producer of premium cigars, in 1994 exporting fifty-two million cigars to the United States alone. Seeds of the Connecticut shade-grown tobacco were imported, and the Honduran wrapper leaf has subsequently taken on a decidedly unique, indigenous flavor–since the Jalapa Valley soil is sweeter than Connecticut's, so is the Honduran wrapper, in much the same way that grapes from vines that travel to California from France take on a slightly new flavor and body in their new land. Today, Honduras is home to leading premium-cigar makers like Bering, Don Tomás, El Rey del Mundo, Hoyo de Monterrey, Punch, and Nat Sherman.

When blue mold killed off about 25 percent of the total Honduran crop in both 1993 and 1995, growers responded by changing their seasons to the hotter months of January and February that discourage the opportunistic disease, which can ruin several acres in the course of a single night.

- **Jamaica:** Even though Jamaican tobacco isn't as famous or as widely used as Dominican or Cuban tobacco, Jamaica is still home to cigar-making factories, including that of one of the world's most reliably excellent brands, Macanudo, made from Jamaican tobacco as well as Dominican. But names can fool you. For instance, after a hurricane leveled its Jamaican factory, the Special Jamaican brand shifted operations to the Dominican Republic.

- **Nicaragua:** Considered by many to be the potential top successor to Cuba as late as the 1970s, Nicaragua's bloody political turmoil choked off the outflow of tobacco altogether in the 1980s, when fields and factories were put to the torch and the Sandinista government endured its own trade embargo by the United States. But the last few years have brought a measure of stability and a more moderate economic philosophy to Nicaragua, and growers and cigar makers in this Central American country are getting their fields and factories back in operation. In their rush to return to world markets, some of the cigars produced recently in Nicaragua have been sold before their time; the 1993 harvest was the first good one in a while. Look for brands like Joyo de Nicaragua and La Finca to once again impress even the most discriminating cigar enthusiast with a well-made, robust, full-bodied product.

- **Canary Islands:** Successful Cuban cigar dynasties, like the Menendez and Garcia families of the Montecristo brand, fled Cuba in the wake of the Castro takeover and wound up in the Canary Islands. Many of them returned to the Caribbean–mostly the Dominican Republic–when they discovered that replicating Cuba's growing conditions in the North Atlantic was difficult, but some brands still manufacture cigars in what the Spaniards call Las Canarias.

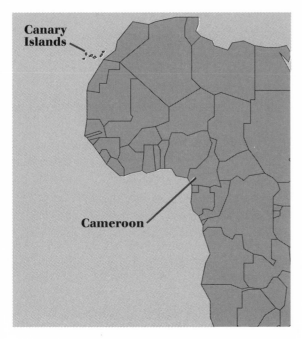

Canary
Islands

Cameroon

■ **Cameroon:** In order to raise a successful tobacco crop, three general factors need to be present–a favorable climate, the proper soil, and the know-how to do the job right. Cameroon, on the Atlantic coast of Africa just north of the equator, has all three.

Tobacco seed was brought to the humid valleys of Cameroon in the early part of the twentieth century by the French, who colonized the country, and the first Cameroon tobacco sold on the international market was auctioned in Paris right after the Second World War. Today, Cameroon wrapper is in great demand and short supply. Consequently, it's among the world's most sought-after tobaccos, renowned for its rich, robust flavor, tasting much like maduro leaves but with a fuller aftertaste and a different appearance. Cameroon wrapper is more of a colorado or colorado-maduro color: that is, light brown with a reddish tinge or darkish brown. Tobacco from Cameroon seeds is held in such high esteem that it's now being grown all over the globe.

■ **Philippines:** The cigar factories of the Philippines have supplied the world market since the nineteenth century. Because of their proximity to the tobacco farms of the island nations of the Indian Ocean, many Filipino brands feature Indonesian or Javanese binder and filler leaves. Good examples of these types of cigars are the Alhambra and Calixto López brands. The latter is made with a Havana-seed wrapper.

■ **Sumatra:** When the Dutch established colonial rule on this Indonesian island very early in the nineteenth century, they brought their tobacco-farming methods with them. Sumatra became a thriving center for the cultivation of the "dry" Dutch-style cigars, and it remains so to this day. Due to Sumatra's historic legacy, few handmade, premium cigar brands originate here, and most of the Sumatra product is machine-rolled and short-filled, either on the Indonesian island itself or back in Holland. Because of this, the Sumatra leaf continues to be more popular in Europe than in the United States.

The Sumatran farmers started their tobacco farms by planting seeds culled from Connecticut shade-grown wrapper plants, and for years their product could be considered an imitation of that world-famous wrapper leaf. Now, however, the Sumatran product looks more and more like the Connecticut product, signaling that years of refinement have been a success.

■ **Brazil:** Though the tobacco industry in Brazil got its start with the Portuguese, who planted Sumatra seed and shipped their best leaf back to Europe starting in the eighteenth century, one firm dominates Brazilian cigar tobacco today–a Dutch family-owned company named Suerdieck. Not only do they oversee the making of ten varieties of handmade cigars and nine machine-made selections under their own brand name, but they produce the Don Pepe and Iracema lines of handmade cigars as well. The four Don Pepe varieties are made of Brazilian filler, binder, and the homegrown wrapper from the aforementioned Sumatra seed; the Iracema features a Connecticut shade-grown wrapper.

Certainly, one of the fun challenges of being involved in the tobacco industry from seedling to cigar is taking part in the exciting enterprise of launching a line of cigars, and some entrepreneurs are looking to turn Brazil into one of the world's foremost growing regions for cigar tobacco. One-time amateur cigar enthusiasts like Herman Upmann and Zino Davidoff turned their passion into profit and enriched the entire cigar-smoking world.

But it might be tougher for these

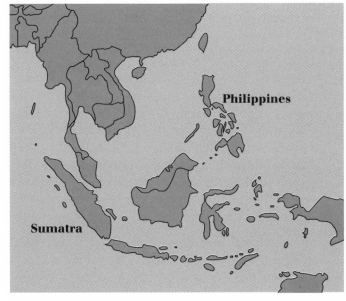

contemporary businesspeople. Not only must they find the right combination of tobaccos to yield the distinctive flavor they're after—which is something of a balancing act, mixing and matching the different varieties available—they have to make sure they can manufacture it in quantities that will satisfy what they hope will be a mad rush by their customers to purchase the new product. This isn't always easy. As a result of the current popularity of premium cigars, there's a shortage of fine tobacco in the world today—good wrapper leaf, especially—and because these entrepreneurs haven't developed decades-long relationships with Caribbean tobacco growers like a lot of us old-time cigar makers have, they'll find it difficult to purchase enough top-notch tobacco to meet the demands of their customers.

So what's a newcomer to the business to do? Well, he can find a farmer in a place like Brazil, who will plant Cuban or Connecticut or Cameroon seed, and take a chance on growing, harvesting, and manufacturing cigars in a new place. Then he can bring a unique product to market under his own brand name. That's what some tobacco entrepreneurs are doing today in Brazil.

Look for more Brazilian tobacco in the cigars available in U.S. tobacco shops in the very near future.

■ **Ecuador:** The foggy weather in this South American country provides natural shade, allowing growers to cultivate a light-colored, mild-flavored wrapper tobacco from Connecticut and Cameroon seed that's just now hitting the international markets. It remains to be seen if Ecuador, with its efficacious growing conditions, can emerge as a powerful and popular center of cigar-tobacco growing in the world.

■ **Mexico:** For years, Mexican tobacco was used for low-cost filler and binder—the one part of the cigar that uses tobacco known only for its tensile strength, and not its flavor or appearance. When Te-Amo came out with its cigar made from all-Mexican tobaccos, a lot of influential people in the cigar industry considered it a substandard product. Te-Amo was inexpensive and, peculiarly, it was popular in only one region—New York City, where it remains ubiquitous to this day. I suppose it took some special capacity to enjoy Te-Amo cigars, handmade in Mexico's San Andrés Valley, and whatever capacity it took was prevalent in the New York area alone.

Unfortunately, Te-Amo isn't popular with everyone, and some cigar smokers thumbed their noses at the whole idea of Mexican cigar tobacco. This

To make it easier for you to select the cigar that's perfect for you, I've divided the following photographs of top-quality handmade cigars into two categories: size and color.

In the following photos, you'll find cigars grouped according to size, starting with the largest cigars on the market. Keep in mind that a cigar is sized according to its length (measured in inches) and its diameter (or ring gauge, measured 64ths of an inch). The biggest cigars, the giants, weigh in at a whopping ten inches in length, with a ring gauge of 66 (just over an inch in diameter). Flip through these pages, and you'll see examples of many of my favorite cigars from the gargantuan down to the panatela, exemplified by the Nat Sherman Academy No. 2, which is five inches long with a ring gauge of 31, meaning it's almost half an inch wide ($^{31}/_{64}$ths).

GIANT, DOUBLE CORONA, CHURCHILL

1 Nat Sherman No. 500
2 Casa Blanca Jereboam
3 Royal Jamaica Double Corona
4 Partagas No. 10
5 Te-Amo Churchill
6 Nat Sherman Hampton
7 Montecristo Churchill
8 J & R Ultimate Double Corona
9 Ashton Gigante

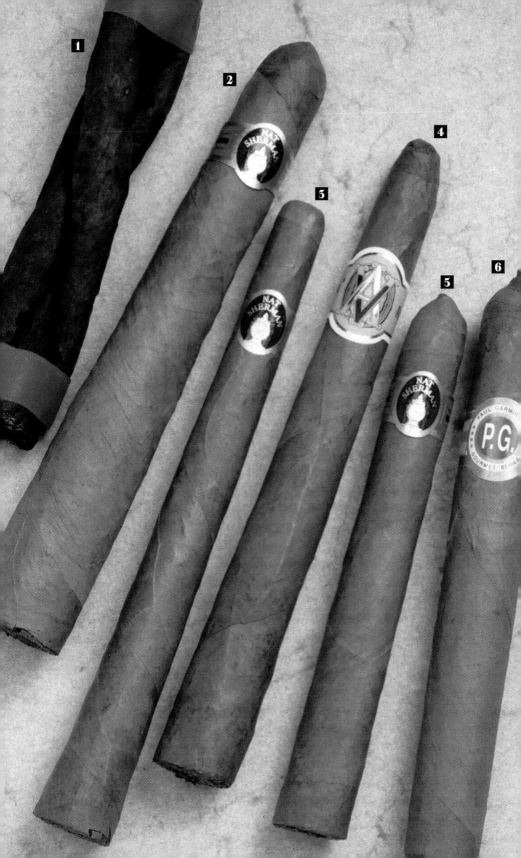

**GRAND CORONA,
CORONA EXTRA,
GIANT CORONA
(MIDDLEWEIGHTS)**

1 J & R Ultimate No. 1
2 Nat Sherman Dispatch
3 Punch Chateau M
4 Ashton No. 3
5 Nat Sherman
   Trafalgar No. 4

**LONSDALE
(*facing page*)**

1 Nat Sherman
   Butterfield No. 8
2 Macanudo Baron
   de Rothschild
3 Licenciados No. 300
4 Nat Sherman
   Algonquin
5 Licenciados
   Excellente
6 Paul Garmirian No. 5

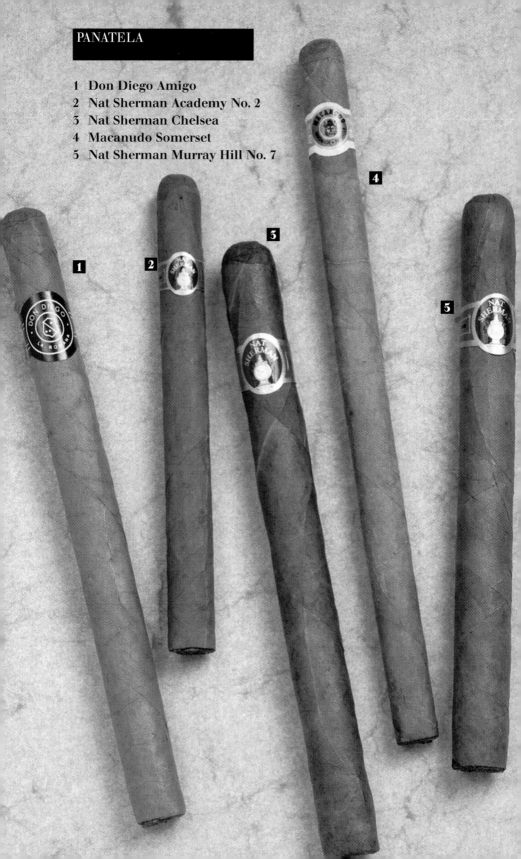

PANATELA

1 Don Diego Amigo
2 Nat Sherman Academy No. 2
3 Nat Sherman Chelsea
4 Macanudo Somerset
5 Nat Sherman Murray Hill No. 7

For those smokers who like to choose their cigars by flavor, I've grouped the following photos of cigars by wrapper color to make your choice that much easier. Keep in mind that wrappers provide about 70 percent of a cigar's flavor. The cigars here are among the best on the market and represent every wrapper type currently available. Remember, nobody can tell you which cigar is the best one for you. Only you can make a decision. These examples are included here so that you'll have a better idea of what to look for.

The photos start with the double-claro cigars, nick-named "candela" or "American Market Selection" because at one time they were very popular in the United States. They are harder to find nowadays, but if you're curious about their light, somewhat tangy taste, by all means give them a try.

From the double claro, cigar wrappers continue to get darker. Next comes the claro (a pale ginger color), then the colorado claro (tawny brown), the colorado (a mild brown), the colorado-maduro (café-au-lait colored), and, finally, the maduro (chocolate brown). You may hear talk of an oscuro cigar (which means "dark" in Spanish), but that wrapper color is usually lumped into the maduro category.

Remember, there's a gamut of choices. Enjoy finding the one that's right for you.

DOUBLE CLARO

1 Macanudo Lord Clairborn Jade
2 J & R Double Corona
3 Arturo Fuente Fancytail
4 Nat Sherman No. 405
5 J & R Ultimate No. 1

1   J & R Special Jamaican A
2   Dunhill Candados
3   J & R Special Jamaican D
4   Dunhill Natural Panatela

COLORADO CLARO

1 Davidoff 4000
2 Nat Sherman Morgan
3 Nat Sherman Carnegie
4 Nat Sherman No. 1400
5 Nat Sherman Oxford No. 5

COLORADO MADURO

1 Nat Sherman Hamilton
2 Nat Sherman Hobart
3 Nat Sherman Beekman
4 Royal Jamaica Corona
5 Nat Sherman Sutton

6 Nat Sherman Dakota
7 Punch After Dinner
8 Partagas No. 1
9 Nat Sherman Hampshire
10 Nat Sherman Harrington

MADURO

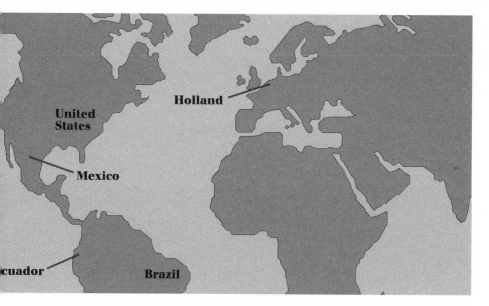

needless prejudice against Mexican leaf persists, which is one reason why being a "connoisseur" isn't always to your advantage–a lot of so-called experts talk themselves out of enjoying some very good cigars.

Like all profit-minded businesspeople, the Mexican growers responded to the changing marketplace and have now been cultivating a premium-quality tobacco for years. And unbeknownst to many of the so-called experts, the tobacco coming out of Mexico today is first-rate. Te-Amo remains Mexico's No. 1 seller in the United States. Truth be told, my current favorite afternoon smoke is from the Nat Sherman Manhattan Selection, which features a Mexican wrapper. I find it smoothly unintrusive to smoke in the middle of the business day, but with enough spice to make it a perfect noontime treat.

■ **Europe:** Though Europe grows almost none of its own tobacco, it stands above other regions of the world in its manufacture of cigars and their consumption. Believe it or not, Denmark is the world's largest consumer per capita of cigars, and Holland is the largest manufacturer of cigars in the world, accounting for nearly half the planet's production–an eye-popping three billion cigars a year.

You won't find any premium-quality handmade cigars coming out of the Netherlands. Instead, the Dutch manufacture the more popular, less expensive, machine-made product, mostly cigarillos, the smallest cigars made (usually less than six inches in length and with a ring gauge of 29 or less). The Dutch raise absolutely no tobacco on their own soil, so the entire industry has been built on imports, mostly tobacco shipped from Sumatra, its former Indonesian colony. The hand-rolling of cigars was a lucrative cottage industry for Dutch families until after the Second World War, when mechanization swallowed the small businesses, and now the Dutch cigar industry is almost all of the machine-made variety. At one time, Amsterdam and Rotterdam were global centers of the trade of imported tobacco, but now all Indonesian tobacco is auctioned in Bremen, Germany, and all Cameroon leaf is sold in Paris.

Accounting for one billion of those machine-made cigars is Agio Sigarenfabrieken, based in the northern Dutch town of Duizel, with factories as far-flung as Malta, Sri Lanka, and the Dominican Republic. Agio ranks as one of the world's most prolific makers of cigarillos, offering their short-filled dry cigars in a wide range of wrapper colors to a voracious European and global market in such well-known varieties as Mehari's and Panter. They have been family-owned and run for generations, with the Winterman brothers, Jack and Ag, at the helm.

As a matter of fact, members of the Winterman family also run another of Holland's top cigar companies, Henri Winterman, which is now owned by British American Tobacco. With sales of six hundred fifty million cigars to some one hundred countries, including the former Soviet Union and its erstwhile satellite nations of Eastern Europe, Winterman ranks third behind Agio and Ebas (sales of nine hundred million) among Dutch companies. A family feud at the turn of the century accounted for the founding of Henri Winterman. Jack and Ag's grandfather and grand-uncle split up, with the grand-uncle establishing Henri Winterman in competition with Agio, and both firms have proved enormously successful through the years.

Another Dutch firm, Schimmelpenninck, which is owned by Rothman's, accounts for about 40 percent of the dry cigars sold in the United States. Their Duet selection is said to be the No. 1-selling cigarillo in the world.

Very few premium-quality handmade cigars are made in Europe. England has just one factory that produces handmade cigars–the Alton Company in Nottingham. And the largest European cigar maker outside of Holland, Nobel of Denmark, sold four hundred million cigars in 1991–all of them the dry variety.

■ **United States:** The sandy soil that lines the banks of the Connecticut River from Hartford north to the Massachusetts state line provides nearly perfect conditions for growing tobacco, and for two hundred years the planters of Connecticut have raised some of the best shade-grown wrapper in the world.

Although the weather in Connecticut allows for only one growing season per year, from March to August, the wrapper is so popular that its presence can add as much as a dollar to the final selling price of a retail cigar. Even so, the supply of Connecticut shade-grown wrapper perennially lags behind demand. Its seeds have traveled around the globe, and there's tobacco being grown as far away as Sumatra and Cameroon with Connecticut seed these days, but none of those tobaccos are able to approach the homegrown variety, which is famous for its light color, its delicate, mild flavor, and its flawless appearance. Nearly all premium-cigar makers around the world use Connecticut shade-grown wrapper.

Though most of the rest of the country is no longer home to all the tobacco crops that prospered in bygone days by catering to the hundreds of local cigar companies, and the Ybor City section of Tampa is now but a shadow of its handmade-cigar glory years, the United States still boasts many successful cigar factories, almost all of them churning out the popular mass-market, machine-made varieties.

The U.S. sales leaders rank among the largest cigar manufacturers in the world. They may be big conglomerates, but the brand names they market are familiar to anyone who's ever been inside a candy store, drugstore, convenience store, or tobacconist shop anywhere in the country. They are Consolidated (nine hundred million cigars sold annually), which makes, among others, Antonio y Cleopatra, Dutch Masters, Muriel, Backwoods, El Producto, Roi-Tan, and Ben Franklin; Swisher International (six hundred million), makers of King Edward, Santa Fe, Swisher Sweets, Optimo, and others; and General Cigar (three hundred fifty million), which makes White Owl, Garcia y Vega, Tijuana Smalls, Robert Burns, and William Penn.

Some well-known names have switched their locations over the years. Phillies, which got its name because it made its cigars in Philadelphia, are now mass-produced in Selma, Alabama, and Garcia y Vega, started in New York City over one hundred years ago, now machine-manufactures its wildly popular cigars in Alabama as well. Others have stayed put. Hav-A-Tampa, which took the domestic market by storm with its Tampa Straights and Tampa Nuggets, is still made in Tampa; Miami is the home of handmade La Gloria Cubanas, not to be confused with the Cuban brand of the same name; the machine-made, long-filled Travis Club line of cigars has

An English-Language Guide to Cigar Boxes

Regardless of where cigars are manufactured, many cigar boxes are stamped with wording that explains *how* the cigars were made. Note the subtle distinction between these three imprints—handmade, hand-rolled, and hand-packed. "Handmade" refers to cigars that are handmade from start to finish; "hand-rolled" refers to machine-bunched cigars that are "finished," or rolled, by hand; and "hand-packed" means that the cigars were completely machine-made but were sorted and arranged by hand. Sometimes, to cater to the vast North American market, cigar makers will stamp their boxes in English, and it'll be easy to tell the differences. But if not, here are some Spanish imprints to be aware of:

■ Hecho a Mano—Made by hand. This usually means the cigars were machine-bunched, then finished by hand, rather than fully handmade.

Cuban manufacturers started using this designation for machine-bunched, hand-finished cigars in 1989. Before that, completely handmade cigars carried this stamp.

■ Totalmente a Mano—Totally by hand. The cigars are handmade from start to finish.

■ Hecho en Mexico—Made in Mexico. Chances are, unless the stamp goes on to say that the cigars were "hecho a mano" or "totalmente a mano," you have a box of machine-made cigars. "Hecho en..." means "Made in...."

■ Envuelto a Mano—Packed by hand. Usually means the cigar itself was made by machine.

Here are some other imprints you're likely to come across. They help you judge a cigar by its box cover. But you should never shell out a lot of money for a box of cigars without having it opened and inspecting it first.

■ Puro—Pure. In the case of Cuban cigars, this stamp accompanies the green-and-white label on the box. It tells you the cigars inside were made of Cuban tobacco and were assembled in Cuba.

■ DC, C, CC, COL, CM, M, or Ma—Refers to the wrapper color of the enclosed cigars. DC stands for double claro, C for claro, CC for colorado claro, COL for colorado, CM for colorado maduro, M and Ma for Maduro.

■ TP—stands for "tobacco product" and is usually followed by a serial number. This means that the cigars were made in the United States.

always been produced in Texas; and White Owl continues its successful run, manufactured in this country since 1887. Two companies that produce handmade cigars are located in highly unlikely places–La Plata has been making cigars in Los Angeles since 1947, and Boquilla still thrives in the Little Havana neighborhood of Union City, New Jersey, far from the inexpensive labor of the Caribbean.

As you can see, though little tobacco is grown here outside the Connecticut River Valley, the United States remains a thriving cigar-making country.

The lucrative U.S. market is also one of the prime targets of cigar makers elsewhere in the world. The leading exporters of cigars to the United States in 1994 were the Dominican Republic (67 million), Honduras (52 million), Jamaica (11 million), Mexico (6 million), and Holland (3 million).

Chapter Three

What to Smoke:
A Guide for the
Enthusiast

Walk into a tobacconist's shop today and
you'll find a dizzying array of cigars for sale.
With some 450 brands on the market—and
some of those brands offering as many as two
or three dozen different varieties—choosing

a single cigar that fits what you're looking for can seem like a daunting task.

Fortunately, finding the right match for you is simpler than it appears. Together we can break down the vertiginous variety of cigars into more manageable parts. I'll help you define what you want, provide you with enough information to clarify what sounds good, and give you some sampling suggestions to get started. When we're done, you'll be able to tell a candela from a maduro with one eye closed, and you'll know at what time of day you'd prefer a Robusto over a Lonsdale. After you've settled on one or two or three different cigars as your favorites, you might find that the real fun was in the hunt. The good news is that the hunt never has to end.

Three questions

Before you begin perusing the options, ask yourself these two questions:

- What flavor do I want from my cigar?

- How much time do I want to take to smoke it?

The answers to these questions will determine the type of cigar you choose—more specifically, the wrapper color and the blend—and will also give you an idea as to the cigar's size.

After you've answered those questions, there's a third one, nearly as important:

- How much money am I willing to spend?

Though the asking prices of most of the cigars we'll discuss won't force you to sell your car in order to afford them, some cigars are more expensive than others. Since prices vary, and tend to fluctuate over even short

---

There are a lot of choices out there: 450 cigar brands compete for the loyalty of the world's smokers.

---

periods of time, I won't talk specific numbers, but I have a rule of thumb: It's just not worth it to go into hock for a cigar. A perfectly good cigar, handmade in the Dominican Republic or Honduras, can be purchased for about three dollars, and most of the cigars I'll be talking about are available for between three and ten dollars each. In addition, I'm sure you'll find, as I have, that in a lot of cases price has very little to do with quality.

Just because one cigar costs three dollars and another costs seven doesn't guarantee you'll enjoy the seven-dollar smoke any better. As a matter of fact, you might often prefer the less costly cigar! Ultimately, there are plenty of worthwhile varieties that are within your price range.

Be warned, however. If you're looking for the one cigar that will satisfy you every time you have the urge to light up, you may be disappointed. Contrary to Rudyard Kipling's famous advice ("A woman is only a woman, but a good cigar is a smoke"), a cigar is not always more satisfying than a lover. Many people do mate for life and settle on one brand and one type of cigar for all time, and perhaps you're one of them; but many more do not. The days of absolute brand loyalty—when a smoker would select a certain cigar and smoke it

---

The same cigar you loved at lunch may be too mild for after dinner.

---

exclusively for twenty years—are for the most part long over. The trend nowadays is to choose three or four types and have them all laid away in the home humidor for breaking out at different occasions. And why not? With such a diversity of premium products now on the market, why not take advantage of the many types available?

Another reason not to set your sights on a single type of cigar as your one and only is the fact that there are so many different factors that go into your enjoyment of a cigar—the day of the week, the time of day, your mood, the company you're with when you light up, the size and shape of the cigar, what you've just eaten or drunk—even the weather. The same cigar you loved at lunch may be too mild for after dinner. The same smoke you savored on Sunday may be too leisurely for the weekday. The very same blend you adored in a full-bodied Double Corona may strike you as too mild in a Panatela. The humidor can be a smorgasbord! Have fun sampling what's available.

How to buy a cigar

I recommend giving certain brands or types of cigars more than just one or two smokes before you buy a box of them. One of the criteria by which cigar makers judge the finer cigars is their consistency, and certainly, the quality can fluctuate–even among cigars from the same box. Therefore, you can't properly judge a cigar by smoking just one or two.

When you buy cigars by the box, you have a right to see the contents before plunking down your cash. Even if you're familiar with the brand, ask the tobacconist to open the box. He should comply readily. Just like a carton of eggs at the grocery store, every box is different, and you don't know when a certain one has not been manufactured to your liking. Take a good look at the cigars lined up inside. Not only is the blend of the cigar's tobacco a good yardstick to use to determine its quality, so is its construction. Make sure their colors are uniform, and there's no damage to the wrappers. If the colors vary too much, the quality-control person at the factory may have been napping. If the colors vary and the box has already been opened, it may mean that the clerks at the tobacco shop have been selling individual cigars out of that box and filling in the blanks with cigars from another. Gently squeeze the middle of a cigar or two. The wrapper should give and then bounce back to its original shape. (Be careful not to damage the wrapper, however!) That means the leaves are still supple. If the cigar makes a crinkly noise or snaps, that means it's dried out. If it sags after you squeeze it, it wasn't properly filled or contains too much

---

Maybe after sampling the handmade brands, you'll go back to smoking Tiparillos.

---

moisture. It will probably not draw very well. Smell the cigar. Don't be timid about selecting a cigar out of the box and taking a whiff. Stick your nose in the place where you took the cigar from–that's where you get a true sense of the aroma. If the bouquet agrees with you, the cigar probably will, too.

Light one up. Consider the draw. Is it hard work drawing the smoke out of the end? If so, the cigar has a "knot," meaning it's been rolled improperly. Does it burn too fast? Problems with inconsistent draw are almost nonexistent in the machine-made varieties, as automation has taken the guesswork out of the equation. Some handmade cigars will prove to be substandard, though this, too, is rare. I'd say perhaps one cigar in the odd box of twenty-five will simply not draw well, or one side of the cigar will burn faster than another. This may be indicative of an uneven bunching of the filler, or some other inconsistency in its rolling. Look for a thin black ring to form around the ash at the end of the cigar. This will indicate that the tobacco has been cured properly.

Finally, consider the flavor and the way the size of the cigar feels in your fingers, in your mouth. Are you comfortable with it? Is the taste of the wrapper to your liking? Does it have a pleasant aftertaste? Can you handle it with ease? Can you get your lips around it? Does the total experience of it appeal to you?

Your first puff

If you're like a lot of American cigar smokers, your first puff was on a Phillie or a Tiparillo. Perhaps you first sampled a White Owl, a Swisher Sweet, or an Antonio y Cleopatra. In any case, your first cigar was probably an inexpensive, machine-made, short-filled cigar from an unhumidified case, like one of those brands, and the experience was pleasant, because why else would you be reading this, your curiosity about cigars piqued and your appetite whetted for more?

Tiparillos, Phillies, and the other domestic cigar brands are the bread and butter of the American cigar industry. Many, many people swear by them, and for a long time sales of these affordable cigars propelled the entire cigar trade. Some of the most avid cigar smokers adore them, and if you enjoy them, too, I think that's great. They are common enough that you'll never have trouble locating them in stores, and they're inexpensive.

If you've smoked these less expensive, mass-market cigars and you're looking to break into the premium varieties, or you're a beginner in the world of cigars, you probably want to start with a lighter cigar. You don't have to spend a lot of money to get a handmade cigar from the Dominican Republic with a smooth Connecticut shade-grown wrapper: for instance, a Nat Sherman Academy No. 2 that will serve as a fine introduction to the handmade types. But I would probably shy away from a cigar with a fuller flavor, like one with a Cameroon wrapper. Like most refined tastes, it takes time to develop a proper palate for the heartier handmade cigars. You don't wake up one morning and, never having smoked a cigar before, suddenly take great pleasure from, say, a Nat Sherman Vanderbilt. It takes time to acquire the taste for it.

So while I'll mention the machine-made cigars, and provide plenty of examples of their different varieties for you to try, for the most part I'll be discussing cigar characteristics that are prevalent along the higher end of the cigar spectrum–the handmade, more expensive premium varieties.

Who knows? Maybe you'll try branching out into the handmade brands of imported cigars and find that you really prefer Tiparillos. There's nothing wrong with that.

As I've stated before, I'm against cigar ratings for that one simple reason: What tastes good to me could taste awful to you, and vice versa. You'll never catch me assigning a rating system to cigars, giving them number grades or stars or even a thumbs-up or -down. You'll never hear me say that one cigar is "better" than another. I can make suggestions about certain cigars, describe their characteristics, offer an opinion on their craftsmanship, but the final judgment is yours. It's up to you to choose the best cigar for you.

Instead of a ratings system, what I'm going to do is this: make it easy for you to select the perfect cigar for yourself. I'll run down the characteristics of the different shapes, sizes, and "colors" of cigars; give you an idea of what they'll taste like; provide you with examples of finer brand names in each category; and give you enough information to make the proper selection based on facts.

I've broken down the world of cigars into two categories–the handmade, more expensive products, and the machine-made mass-market variety. Within those classifications, I've further divided them by size and wrapper color, and offered some of the well-made examples of each size.

You can use this guide in two different ways: Thumb through the sizes and decide which one appeals to you, then sample a cigar I suggest in a particular size group, or select your cigar by wrapper color, which determines the major part of its flavor. Flavor or size–take your pick.

I've included photos of some of the different varieties of cigar on the market today so it'll be easy for you to walk into a tobacco shop and know what to look for. When you hit on a category of cigar that arouses your interest, take a look at the picture of it in the full-color insert. If it catches your eye, try it.

While I list the premium brands and the mass-market brands side by side, keep in mind that a vast difference exists between them. The premium cigars have been fashioned by hand, with extreme care taken from the time the tobacco was a seedling to the time it's sold to you from the store's humidor. By contrast, many of the mass-market varieties aren't made of whole-leaf tobacco, but rather a tobacco-and-vegetable substance called homogenized tobacco, manufactured so as to facilitate mass production. Though I would never tell you that one is "better" than the other–everybody's taste is different–there's no doubt that the craftsmanship and skill that goes into the premium cigar more than justifies its higher price.

Guide to cigars by size

My father, Nat, who sold hundreds of thousands of cigars in his day, used to say that people "wear" a fine cigar. As far as cigars go, size really does matter. Not only will the same blend of tobaccos taste differently depending on the size, but your personal comfort level with the size and shape of a cigar goes a long way toward determining your enjoyment of the product.

Cigars are sized two ways–length and diameter. The length of the cigar is specified in inches and the diameter is calculated by what's called ring gauge. Ring gauge is measured in 64ths of an inch. For example, the cigar I'm smoking today, the Nat Sherman Chelsea, is 6½ x 38, meaning that it's 6½ inches long and 38⁄64ths of an inch in diameter, or just over a half-inch wide. Most cigars have ring gauges of between 28 and 50. (Cigarettes, to give you a comparison, generally have a width the equivalent of a ring gauge of 20.) Because the cigar industry is a colorful one and loves nicknames, every size and shape has a special designation, and a cigar of my Chelsea's length and width is called a panatela. I'll explain more about that later.

You can be your own custom tailor, fitting the right cigar to your build, personality, and preferences. Here are some hints to get you started:

■ Length and ring gauge have a major effect on the flavor of a cigar. The same cigar you just rejected may be perfect for you in a different size. An important rule of thumb is that the wider the ring gauge, the fuller the flavor of the cigar. If you prefer a lighter smoke, start with a smaller ring gauge. If you're in the mood for a full-bodied, robust, intensely flavorful cigar, try one with a wide ring gauge.

50 RING

49 RING

48 RING

47 RING

46 RING

44 RING

- The right size for you is the one you feel most comfortable with and that fits you. What does it mean to be "comfortable" with a cigar? If it's too wide to get your mouth around, you're probably better off with a smaller ring gauge. If you find the taste of a certain cigar too light, try a model with a wider ring gauge.

- Take into account the amount of time you want to devote to your cigar. For instance, if I'm smoking during the day, I prefer a shorter cigar with a large ring gauge so I can enjoy a robust, eye-opening flavor in a cigar that can be finished in a relatively short time. Keep in mind that once a cigar has cooled and its oils have crystallized, it can no longer be smoked. So if you can't save a half-smoked cigar for later, what good is lighting up a big, fat cigar if you only have a few minutes to smoke it? I think it detracts from my enjoyment of a cigar to always be checking my watch while I'm puffing away.

- If you're giving a gift and don't know what the recipient smokes, play it safe in the middle size ranges. Or you can try and fit the cigar to the smoker's personality–larger for the extroverted; smaller for the shy–and size–wider for the stouter person; longer and thinner for the taller and lankier.

- A cigar with a larger ring gauge will generally burn cooler–meaning your fingers and lips won't feel the heat as much–and deliver more flavor per puff. Keep in mind: In general, the smaller the ring, the lighter the smoke.

Name that fume

Most names for cigar sizes were started within the industry by manufacturers who were looking for a shorthand way of referring to certain lengths and ring gauges without always having to mention the specific numbers. Or some influential person in history popularized the size and hence became eponymously linked to that certain cigar type.

I've never been one to go up and down lists like this one and memorize the different nicknames for the different sizes of cigars; I'm more of the

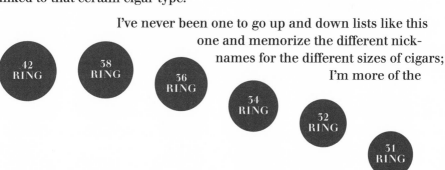

42 RING
38 RING
36 RING
34 RING
32 RING
31 RING
28 RING

I-know-what-I-like school. But I think it's instructive for you to familiarize yourself with the various nicknames to get a sense of the color of the cigar industry. Plus, you'll be able to walk into a cigar store and ask for a Lonsdale if that's what you want. Keep in mind, however, that none of the following names are written in stone. Sizes in each category have a tendency to shift somewhat over time, and different manufacturers use different names for the different sizes. For example, one manufacturer will call a certain line of cigars Churchills when its size, according to industry standards and a majority of cigar makers, is more of a Double Corona.

A caveat: Due to fluctuations in the market, whims of the cigar manufacturers, political conditions in the cigars' nations of origin, and possible early senescence on my part, not all of the individual cigars I'll be naming in the following pages will be available on your tobacconist's shelves. This is an unfortunate inevitability of both the laws of supply and demand and the guide-writing business. At best, you'll be able to find exactly what you're looking for the first time and every time; at worst, you'll be able to use this guide as a compass—it'll point you in the right direction, and you can take it from there.

All models listed below have parallel sides, capped head, and an open end unless otherwise indicated.

The big boys

A great majority of the largest varieties of cigars fall into the handmade category, and their size can generally provide smoking companionship for an hour or more, with their wide ring gauges guaranteeing a full-flavored smoke.

■ **Giant:** The largest cigars on the market, giants are the heavyweight division of cigars and measure anywhere over 8 inches long with a ring gauge of greater than 50, with a 9 x 52 cigar being about the norm. These are mostly gimmick items and are not terribly easy to handle or to smoke.

The distinction of being the widest and longest cigar in general production today is a tie between two models named the General, both boasting an Ecuadorian wrapper and handmade in Honduras by the Cuba Aliados and Puros Indios brands. These bombers measure an astounding 18 inches long and have a ring gauge of 66—more than an inch wide. I caution you: Don't light up these Generals unless you have a couple of days in which to smoke them!

The Philippines-based cigar maker Tabacalera offers what it calls a Gigante ("giant" in Spanish), which measures in at a hefty 14¼ x 60, and Mexican Emperador produces a handmade cigar using all-Mexican tobacco that measures 13¾ inches in length but boasts a more manageable ring gauge of 49.

Others in the giants-of-the-giants category include the King No. 9 (10 x 66); the Cibao Magnum (10 x 50); the Casa Blanca Jereboam (10 x 66); the Figurin by both Cuba Aliados and Puros Indios (10 x 60); and the Fat Tub, manufactured by Dominican Original (10 x 66). Could you walk up to a tobacconist's counter and say, with a straight face, "Give me a Fat Tub, please"?

■ **Double Corona:** Before Winston Churchill came along—he of the two hundred fifty thousand cigars smoked during his lifetime—a cigar that measured between 6¾ inches and 7¾ inches with a ring gauge between 49 and 54 was called a Double Corona (*corona* is Spanish for "crown"). Over time, what we refer to these days as a Churchill evolved into a slightly smaller variety.

A typical Double Corona is 7¾ x 49. The Nat Sherman No. 500, from our Gotham series, measures 7 x 49 and provides a light flavor for a cigar this big.

Three of the world's most famous cigar brands have some nice examples of cigars in this range: the Excalibur No. 1, handmade in Honduras with either a colorado-claro or maduro Ecuadorian wrapper by Hoyo de Monterrey (7¼ x 54); the Punch Grand Cru Diadema (7¼ x 52), also handmade in Honduras, with a colorado wrapper; and Arturo Fuente's Dante (7 x 52), with a lighter Connecticut shade-grown wrapper.

The Fuente family, incidentally, has been in the cigar trade since the nineteenth century, starting in Cuba, shifting operations to Florida in the early 1900s, and, after stints in Puerto Rico, Nicaragua, and Honduras, settling finally in the Dominican Republic in 1980, where at first they employed just seven people in their factory. Today, six of those folks are reportedly still working for Arturo Fuente—along with more than 500 others—and they produce eighteen million cigars annually. Other brands, such as the well-respected Ashton label, come out of the Fuente factory as well.

■ **Churchill:** The typical Churchill measures 7 inches and has a 48 ring gauge, with a range of 7⅞ to 6¾ inches and a ring gauge of 46 to 48.

There's no doubt that the first Churchill cigar got its name as a shrewd marketing ploy by some enterprising tobacconist who sought to play on the fame of England's wartime prime minister, famous for his ever-present cigar and his flashing of the "V" sign for victory. My father, Nat, claimed he had the real scoop. During the Second World War, Winston Churchill was visiting New York, and as usual he brought along his personal supply of

You don't have to be a millionaire to enjoy a premium handmade cigar.

Double Coronas, as they were called at the time, so Nat's store on Broadway wasn't part of his itinerary, though Nat surely wished it were. One rainy night Churchill, being tired and, after all, British, rushed across 57th Street without watching for traffic on the right side of the street. He was struck by a cab. While he recovered in a Manhattan hospital, Nat hung a sign in his store window that read GET WELL, CHURCHILL, by sheer coincidence behind a display of Double Coronas that were suddenly in great demand, and people started asking Nat for his "Churchills."

Though this tale has the usual ring of truth that most of my father's stories about those days do, it's not known for certain where and when the Churchill got its name. Whatever the true wellspring of the sobriquet, Churchills are still in great demand. I think their length—which keeps them going for a long time—combined with a larger, easy-to-handle ring gauge, makes them so popular. Nat Sherman offers a Churchill in a number of different blends—the full-bodied maduro Dakota, the Honduran-made Hampton, and the smoother Oxford No. 5 with a Connecticut wrapper.

Partagas makes a quality Dominican-made Churchill—the No. 10 (7½ x 49), which features a spicy colorado-maduro wrapper made of Cameroon tobacco. On the lighter side, the Montecristo Churchill, also handmade in the Dominican Republic, is a stellar example of a Churchill (7 x 48) with a subtler, smoother Connecticut shade-grown wrapper, as is the Churchill (also 7 x 48) made by a relative newcomer to the industry, Honduran-based V Centennial, which uses a four-tobacco blend in its filler. Another noteworthy cigar of this size is the Honduran-made El Rey del Mundo Double Corona (7 x 48).

Figurados

Figurados are known more for their distinctive shapes than they are for their particular range of sizes, and owing to their unique construction, they usually number among the longer and bigger cigars. Figurados are all "shaped" cigars with conical ends, and varying dimensions. Great skill is needed to roll these cigars, and typically a cigar factory foreman will assign his best and most experienced rollers to the task. Figurados fall into three main categories and a special one.

■ **Pyramid:** A cigar with a ring gauge that increases continuously from a narrow head to a wide foot is called a Pyramid. You might hear them referred to as "trumpets," and they do remind me of a horn, though I think they look more like clarinets. Pyramids usually measure 7 inches long or shorter, with a ring gauge that necessarily changes from, say, a 36 to a 54 down its length. Length and ring size vary a great deal.

Nat Sherman makes three Pyramids, all from our Metropolitan collection, in which every cigar is named after a famous private club in Manhattan. They are Explorers (5½ inches long with a ring gauge that starts at 44 and widens to 56), Nautical (7 x 34 to 48), and the big Metropolitan (7 x 47 to 60). The Puros Indios brand makes two Pyramids–Piramide No. 1 and Piramide No. 2–with colorado wrappers from Ecuador, and they both feature a very small, pointed tip. Avo, a line of handmade Dominican cigars founded by the musician-turned-cigar-maker Avo Uzevian, makes a Pyramid called the Intermezzo with a Connecticut shade-grown wrapper, and in all these models you can tell the superior craft that's gone into fashioning the small head and the gently tapered sides.

Another variation on the narrower head is called a "fancytail." It's when the cigar roller twists the head of the cigar, creating a kind of pigtail coil of tobacco at the cigar's crown that must be cut off before the cigar can be smoked. At one time, rollers who were making cigars for themselves didn't want to go to the trouble of affixing a cap, so they just gave the head a twist between their fingers, and now it's considered something of a special, elegant feature.

Nat Sherman makes the Zigfeld (6¾ x 38) with a Connecticut wrapper and a fancytail, which is closed at both the head and the end. You can tell if such a cigar has been well-made when you light it. Instead of the flame at the end of the cigar shooting up like it does with other cigar varieties, the flame shoots out, like a flamethrower, when the end wrapper is burned through. The Juan Clemente Especial (a Long Panatela at 7½ x 38), with its mellow Connecticut colorado wrapper, is also a fancytail.

As an aside, the Juan Clemente story is an interesting one. Here was a Frenchman, Jean Clement, who so loved cigars that he started his own brand in the Dominican Republic in the 1980s. The company eschews the industry-wide use of bands that gird the cigar close to its crown end. Instead, the band is attached to the foot of a Juan Clemente cigar.

Speaking of innovation, the practice of wrapping the end of the cigar in foil was another brainchild of my father, Nat Sherman. When he first got started in the cigar business, back in 1928, he bought a stake in the Epoca cigar factory in Tampa, and they made cigars with foil on the end. Soon, with the Depression on, it wasn't economically justifiable to make a cigar with a foiled end, and then the war came and the aluminum was needed for the war effort. But in the early 1950s, Nat revived the silver-tipped cigars with his Nat Sherman 400 series. He was careful to have the words PATENT PENDING printed on the band, to scare off any imitators. But he never did get the thing patented!

■ **Torpedo or Belicoso:** A cigar with a conical head that flares out to wider sides that maintain a constant ring gauge to the foot is called a Torpedo, or Belicoso in the Spanish parlance. One of the advantages of the Torpedo is that you can enjoy a larger ring gauge without worrying about being uncomfortable getting the wide end between your teeth–the Torpedo's crown acts almost like a mouthpiece.

The cigars really do look like missiles, so the derivation of the name "torpedo"–in Spanish, *belicoso* means belligerent or warlike–is obvious. But don't let that fool you. Paul Garmirian makes its Belicoso (6¼ x 52) in the Dominican Republic with a Connecticut shade-grown wrapper that's as mellow as any cigar you'll find.

■ **Perfecto:** A Perfecto is a cigar with a cone-shaped head and foot. These are rare nowadays, though they were at one time much more common. They are thicker in the middle, with a similar-width head and foot. An example of a Perfecto would be the cigars of the Ashton Aged Cabinet Selection, which is available in three big sizes–Giant, Churchill, and Double Corona.

■ **Culebra:** It's also worth mentioning another, special kind of cigar, three cigars coiled together and attached to one another by a band that surrounds all three.

There are two stories that attempt to explain the origin of this peculiar product. Some say that old-time rollers were allowed to bring home three cigars a day for their personal consumption, and the act of twisting them together while they were still wet would make detection of unauthorized cigars leaving the factory premises an easy task.

Another explanation is that the Cuban cigar makers were sick of counterfeiters who sold what they claimed was a handmade Cuban product to visiting sailors when what was really being offered by the crooks was a dry, short-filled cigar of questionable quality. In order to distinguish between the dry product of the counterfeiters and the humidified, handmade cigars of the Cuban factories, the cigars were coiled into threes. Only the humid, long-filled product was twistable in that way. Given the same treatment, the counterfeit short-filled cigars would crack and be ruined.

In any event, the Culebra, which means "snake" in Spanish, is still being sold today. Hoyo de Monterrey (Honduras) and Calixto López (Philippines) are among the current manufacturers of Culebras.

Nat Sherman makes a Culebra, too, and has done so for years. When pop singer Chubby Checker started the Twist dance craze in the early 1960s, my father, who always seemed to be in the right place at the right time, was photographed for *Life* magazine puffing on a twisted cigar. It was great publicity for the store.

If you've never seen a Culebra, ask your tobacconist to show you one. Be sure to take them apart and light them up one at a time. They're such an unusual sight that smoking them is almost an afterthought. Almost.

In-between sizes

These cigars are more varied in their ring gauges than the larger types, and depending on their size they can be enjoyed, generally speaking, anywhere from forty-five minutes to more than an hour. These sizes include many machine-made cigars as well.

■ **Toro:** Kind of an in-between proportion, the Toro (which means "bull" in Spanish) can measure anywhere from 5⅝ to 6⅝ inches, with a ring gauge between 48 and 54. I've always thought of Toros as simply Churchills that measured on the small side, but the trend in the industry is toward more specific labeling of the product, so if anyone asks, they're Toros.

Nat Sherman's Toros run the gamut of cigar taste. The No. 711 (6 x 50) has a mellow colorado-claro wrapper, and the Telegraph (6 x 50) features a much heartier maduro wrapper.

A typical Toro is the Dominican handmade Onyx No. 650, which measures 6 x 50. The Onyx is a relatively new all-maduro series, with a Mexican wrapper and a pleasant spiciness. The exceptional Arturo Fuente Double Chateau (6¾ x 50), available in colorado claro or maduro, is sold in a paper-thin wrapping of cedar. An example of a lighter-bodied Toro is Dunhill's Condado (6 x 48), with a claro Connecticut wrapper and Dominican and Brazilian filler.

J.R. Famous, the exclusive handmade brand of Lew Rothman's very successful mail-order business and chain of J.R. Tobacco stores, offers the Churchill (5¾ x 50) in either a claro, colorado-maduro, or maduro wrapper. J.R. calls it a Churchill, but contemporary nomenclature deems it a Toro. You see why it can be confusing?

■ **Robusto:** Also known as a Rothschild, this short, wide cigar dates from the 1880s, when British banker Leopold de Rothschild asked the Havana cigar maker Hoyo de Monterrey to roll a short cigar with a large ring gauge so he could enjoy the strong flavor of the wide gauge without taking too much time out from the hectic daily grind of high finance.

Turns out Rothschild had a terrific idea. Perfect for a hearty daytime smoke, the Robusto delivers the full-bodied flavor of a Churchill or a Double Corona, but because it's shorter, you won't spend too much time with it. If you have a leisurely twenty minutes in the middle of the day to catch up on your reading or just kick back and relax between appointments, this may be an ideal cigar. It typically measures 4½ to 5½ inches long with a ring gauge range equal to that of a Double Corona, from 48 to 54.

The Astor (4½ x 50), made by Nat Sherman in the Dominican Republic, has a smooth Connecticut wrapper. Hoyo de Monterrey, now based in Honduras, still makes its Rothschild, in three different wrappers–double claro, colorado claro, and maduro. El Rey del Mundo's Rothschilde (5 x 50), with its Honduran colorado-maduro wrapper, is a good example of a robust Robusto. Romeo y Julieta Vintage makes a milder Robusto in a colorado-claro wrapper. And Temple Hall, a Jamaica-based brand, offers two well-made Robustos, both in a medium-bodied Connecticut colorado-claro wrapper.

Florida-based El Producto–which was the late George Burns's favorite brand–offers two machine-made cigars in the Robusto range–the light-wrapper Favoritas (5 x 48½) and the Escepcionales (5⅛ x 52½).

Middleweight contenders

The next three sizes are named after the Corona, or crown, a size that at one time sat on the large end of the cigar scale. Nowadays, the Corona is one of the smallest of the mostly handmade cigar types.

■ **Grand Corona:** Typically sized between 5⅝ and 6⅝ inches, with a ring gauge range of 45 to 47, the Grand Corona is the same diameter as the Corona Extra but is a longer version.

Nat Sherman's Trafalgar No. 4–reputed to be popular around the White House these days–is a smooth smoke at 6 x 47. For a fuller-bodied cigar, there's the Nat Sherman Dispatch (6½ x 46) with a maduro wrapper.

The Ashton No. 3 (6 x 46), made by world-famous manufacturer Arturo Fuente, is a specially aged selection with a light Connecticut wrapper and Dominican filler and is a fine example of a Grand Corona. A fuller-tasting Grand Corona is available from J.R. Ultimate, which offers what they call a Corona (5⅝ x 45), handmade in Honduras completely from Honduran tobacco, in every shade of wrapper from claro to maduro. J.R. packages the Corona in cedar-lined aluminum tubes.

■ **Corona Extra:** The size of the Corona Extra ranges between 4½ and 5½ inches, with a ring gauge of 45 to 47.

H. Upmann, one of the old-time Cuban cigar makers now produced in the Dominican Republic, makes a Corona Extra with the confusing name Pequeño No. 200 (*pequeño* means "small" in Spanish), which measures 4½ x 46. It has a colorado-maduro wrapper from Sumatra that gives it a well-rounded, medium-bodied flavor. For those of you who like to sample the same model cigar in different-colored wrappers, Punch, a Cuban firm transplanted to Honduras, offers a Corona Extra in its Chateau "M"–available in double claro, colorado maduro, and maduro.

On the mass-market side, both Dutch Masters and Muriel make popular cigars in the Corona Extra size. Dutch Masters' Belvedere (4⅞ x 46½), a short-filled cigar with homogenized binder, features a colorado-maduro wrapper; Muriel's Magnum (4⅝ x 46½) is the Puerto Rico-based manufacturer's largest size offering. It comes in a lighter colorado-claro wrapper.

■ **Giant Corona:** A little longer and a little narrower than the Grand Corona and the Corona Extra, the Giant Corona is so named because its length extends outward from 7½ inches, but its ring gauge is 42 to 45.

Dominican Republic-based Pléiades produces a handmade Giant Corona called the Neptune (7½ x 42) with a colorado-claro wrapper grown in Connecticut and a Dominican filler. The robust flavor typical of this size is offset by the use of well-cured tobaccos and the lightening qualities of the mild wrapper leaf.

Triple crown

The Lonsdale and the three Coronas are among the most popular sizes of cigar today, and it's easy to see why. Their range of ring gauges, 40 to 44, guarantees easy handling, and their lengths, anywhere from 5 to 6½ inches, provide enough tobacco for a solid half hour of smoking.

Lonsdale: England's Earl of Lonsdale took a page out of Rothschild's book when he requested a special shape of cigar from Cuba's Rafael Gonzalez. This was some years after the success of the Rothschild, and Gonzalez eagerly complied, even putting the earl's picture on the inside of the Lonsdale box. Despite the Communist takeover of the Cuban cigar industry, the bourgeois aristocrat's visage was portrayed on Rafael Gonzalez boxes until quite recently.

Today, the Lonsdale lives on. Nearly every manufacturer of hand-made cigars in the world offers its version of the 6½-inch-by-42-ring-gauge cigar, and many mass-market producers do, too. And every wrapper in the color spectrum is represented. Here's a partial listing of brands available in the Lonsdale size, by wrapper type, with the names of the selections in parenthesis.

DOUBLE CLARO: Punch (After Dinner), Hoyo de Monterrey (No. 1), Pléiades (Centaurus), and Bering (Casino).

CLARO: Mocha Supreme (Lord), Dunhill (Diamante), and the Dominican-made Cohiba (Corona Especiale).

COLORADO CLARO: Zino (Mouton-Cadet No. 1), Paul Garmirian (P.G. Lonsdale), Nat Sherman (Butterfield No. 8 and Morgan), Montecristo (No. 1), and Maria Mancini (Grandee).

COLORADO: Juan Clemente (No. 3) and Avo (No. 1).

COLORADO MADURO: Nat Sherman (Algonquin, Gramercy, Hunter, and Harrington), H. Upmann (No. 2000), Te-Amo (Celebration), Ramón

Allones (Crystal), Partagas (8-9-8), El Rey del Mundo (Cedar), Diana Silvius (Diana Corona), Bauzá (Jaguar), and Davidoff (Grand Cru No. 1).

MADURO: Macanudo (Baron de Rothschild), Licenciados (No. 300), the Nicaraguan-made La Finca (Romeo), J.R. Ultimate (Cetro), Cuesta-Rey (No. 1884), Ashton (No. 30), and Arturo Fuente (Spanish Lonsdale).

The brands of mass-market cigars available in the Lonsdale size include the Figaro (Figaro) and Travis Club (Centennial), a long-filled, machine-made cigar manufactured in the United States.

■ **Long Corona:** Lop a half inch off a Lonsdale and what do you have? A Long Corona.

Nat Sherman manufactures a Long Corona in a maduro wrapper (Gazette) and one in a colorado-claro Connecticut shade-grown wrapper (No. 1400). Some other examples are the highly regarded Romeo y Julieta Vintage I, with a Connecticut colorado-claro wrapper and Dominican filler, measuring 6 x 43; and the Dominican-made, medium-bodied Licenciados Excellente (6¼ x 43) with a colorado-maduro Connecticut wrapper and Dominican filler.

Machine-made Long Coronas are manufactured by Garcia y Vega (in two tubed varieties: Gran Corona, which has a double-claro wrapper, and Gran Premio, which features a colorado-claro wrapper); Optimo (its Admiral selection is available in double claro or colorado claro, and its Palmas have a maduro wrapper); and Phillies (Titan).

■ **Corona:** Coronas range from 5¼ to 5¾ inches in length, with ring gauges from 40 to 44. There are many choices of handmade Coronas on the market these days.

Nat Sherman makes two Coronas in a colorado-maduro wrapper: the Hampshire (5½ x 42) and the Hamilton (5½ x 42). Some other good examples include the La Finca Corona (5½ x 42), which is made exclusively with Nicaraguan tobacco and has a colorado-maduro wrapper; the Dominican-made Montesino Diplomatico (5½ x 42), with a colorado Connecticut wrapper; and the Punch Café Royal (5⅝ x 44), with a colorado wrapper grown in Ecuador.

For many mass-market cigar makers, the Corona marks the top end of their size catalog, and just about all the better-known brand names feature it.

■ **Petit Corona:** The typical Petit Corona is between 4 and 5 inches long, with the same range of ring gauges as its cousins, the Corona and the Lonsdale, 40 to 44.

The Ramón Allones D (5 x 42) is a very well-made, full-bodied Petit Corona made in the Dominican Republic with a colorado-maduro wrapper from Cameroon and a Dominican-Mexican filler mix. Paul Garmirian's P.G. No. 2 (4¾ x 48) is a more subtle smoke, with a reddish Connecticut shade-grown wrapper. Its cousin, Garmirian's P.G. No. 5, is at the smallest end of the Petit Corona spectrum, measuring 4 x 40–almost a miniature version of a Robusto.

The Ramón Allones and Paul Garmirian brands offer an interesting contrast–the Ramón Allones line was founded in Cuba in 1837, making it the second-oldest Cuban cigar company, while P.G. cigars were introduced one hundred fifty-three years later, in 1990. The Ramón Allones brand is still being made in Cuba, but the original operation was moved to the Dominican Republic after the Castro revolution.

Long and lanky

Panatelas and cigarillos are far and away the most popular sizes of cigars today. Nearly every manufacturer of both handmade and machine-made products offers a line of the slim, easy-to-handle, easy-to-carry cigar types.

These small cigars are made to smoke anytime. They're typically less demanding of the smoker's attention than the bigger, bolder varieties, and they don't last nearly as long as the big boys. They offer a quicker, lighter smoke.

The vast majority of these smaller types of cigars are machine-made, simply because it's a lot more difficult to hand-roll small cigars. Years ago, hand-rollers for Partagas in Cuba used a wire not much thicker than a paper clip to roll the smaller cigars around. After the cigar was finished, the wire was removed. This not only served as an aid to the roller, it also ensured a smooth draw for the smoker.

The smaller cigars are also popular with women, whose appreciation of cigars has, in general, skyrocketed in recent years. While many women are enjoying the larger, wider varieties, many more prefer their cigars thin and elegant.

■ **Long Panatela:** At 7-plus inches and a ring gauge of 35 to 39, the Long Panatela is a graceful cigar that can last the casual smoker up to thirty minutes.

La Plata, a brand that has the unique distinction of being handmade in Los Angeles, where it's been located since 1947, manufactures a Long Panatela called the Reina (7 x 34), available in a colorado-claro or a maduro wrapper, with what could be termed a United Nations filler–Dominican, Ecuadorian, Honduran, and Mexican tobaccos. H. Upmann makes a Long Panatela it calls El Prado (7 x 36). It features a Sumatran colorado-maduro wrapper and the famous Upmann smoothness.

The Tampa-made Elegante offers the hand-finished Panatela Larga with a colorado-claro Connecticut wrapper, and the Balboa brand out of Panama makes a Long Panatela it calls Palma Extra, available in a full-bodied colorado-claro wrapper or an even heavier maduro. Both the Panatela Larga and the Palma Extra measure a svelte 7 x 36.

■ **Panatela:** Everybody from Avo to Zino makes a panatela, and it's no wonder–they're the most popular size cigar on the market today. Measuring between 5½ and 6⅞ inches with a ring range of 35 to 39, the panatela can be a short but profound smoke, easy on the wallet and effortless to transport.

Credit the Dutch

Mass-market manufacturers dominate trade in the cigars that fit into the Short Panatela and smaller categories. These smaller cigars are wildly popular in Europe and elsewhere abroad, thanks in great measure to the influence of the Dutch, who've been making and expertly marketing the slim, dry cigars for going on 400 years.

■ **Short Panatela:** These stubbier versions of the panatela measure between 4 and 5⅜ inches, with ring gauges between 35 and 39; 5 x 38 is the typical length and width.

Handmade versions of the Short Panatela are offered by Macanudo, whose Caviar (4 x 36) is exquisitely made; Arturo Fuente, whose Petit Corona (5 x 38) comes in a colorado-claro or maduro wrapper; Flor de Nicaragua (Petit, 5½ x 38) a company who's made a bold attempt to produce an all-Nicaraguan cigar, but due to recent shortages of quality homegrown wrapper were forced to use Ecuadorian leaf; and Hoyo de Monterrey, whose Demitasse (4 x 39) is available in a double claro, colorado claro, or maduro.

Machine versions include United States-made Caribbean Rounds (Petites), Directors (Panatela), and King Edward (Panatela Deluxe).

■ **Slim Panatela:** Longer but with a smaller ring gauge, the Slim Panatela averages 6 x 34, with any length longer than 5 inches and ring gauges between 30 to 34 falling within this size.

Among the machine-made varieties in this size are As You Like It (No. 35), Bances (Havana Holder), Budd Sweet (Panatela), Celestino Vega (Classic

Stogie), Dutch Masters (Cameroon Elite), Garcia y Vega (six varieties), William Penn (Panatela), and White Owl (Ranger).

■ **Small Panatela:** Small Panatelas measure 4 to 5 inches long, with ring gauges between 30 and 34, the average being 5 x 33.

Bonita (4½ x 30) and Platinum (4⅞ x 32), manufactured in Honduras by Baccarat Havana Selection, are examples of mild, handmade Honduran Small Panatelas. They taste a bit on the sweet side. Nat Sherman's Academy No. 2 (5 x 31) is made with a colorado-claro Connecticut wrapper. Bering, an old Ybor City company that was founded in 1905 and was taken over by the giant tobacco firm Swisher International, makes a machine-bunched, hand-finished Small Panatela in Honduras it calls the No. 8 (4¼ x 32), which features a smooth and spicy Honduran colorado-claro wrapper. And the Nat Sherman Academy No. 2 (5 x 31) combines a colorado-claro Connecticut shade-grown wrapper with a Dominican filler for a smooth, sophisticated flavor.

Zino, the company founded by and named after the famed international cigar entrepreneur Zino Davidoff, produces premium handrolled cigars in the Dominican Republic and Honduras. Zino also machine-produces a Small Panatela called Por Favor in Brazil. Zino has other mass-market facilities in the Netherlands and Switzerland, where the late Davidoff oversaw his retail store in Geneva for decades. Lancer's Havana Slim is a rare 100-percent tobacco version of a machine-made Small Panatela, and El Producto offers its Little Corona. Other United States-based mass-market brands include Hav-A-Tampa (Cheroot and Junior), Muriel (eight varieties), Swisher Sweets (Outlaw), Tampa Nugget (Junior and Miniature), and Tampa Sweet (Cheroot).

■ **Cigarillo and Cheroot:** These varieties are as small as cigars go. Any smaller and you're flirting with cigarette territory.

While the name cigarillo simply means "small cigar" in Spanish, to me the very mention of the name cheroot conjures images of the wild American West and cowboys chomping on dark, rough-rolled, twiglike cigars that were only a grade above a plug of chewing tobacco. Curiously, the word cheroot has a South Asian origin. It means "curl" in the Tamil language, which is spoken in Sri Lanka. I have no idea how this metamorphosed into a name for a square-cut little cigar, but it did. I think the Dutch must be behind this. Their expert entrepreneurial spirit was responsible for spreading the popularity of their small, dry cigars all around the globe, and some Dutch cigar makers have even farmed out their labor to places like Sri Lanka, making a cultural exchange possible.

Cigarillos and cheroots generally have the same proportions: They measure 6 inches or less, with a ring gauge of 29 or less, and the typical model is about a 4 x 26. These small cigars are immensely popular in dry form in Europe and elsewhere both inside and outside the United States.

There's a big difference between the Dutch-type cigars and the domestic-made smaller machine-made cigars. The Dutch cigars are made dry and meant to be smoked dry. Most of them have no binder whatsoever. By contrast, the American-made smaller cigars are patterned after the larger Caribbean cigars. As such, they're meant to be humidified and are frequently packaged in tubes, cellophane, or other devices that help keep the moisture in. They also have binder, though it's mostly homogenized.

Agio, the Dutch company that sells a mind-boggling one billion dry machine-made cigars a year, makes more cigarillos than anyone, but the world's No. 1-selling individual cigarillo selection is the Duet (5⅝ x 27), made by another Dutch firm, Schimmelpenninck.

Here in the New World, manufacturers offer some unique products. Pennsylvania-based Backwoods, made by Consolidated Cigar, produces a cigarillo which is sold in bunches of eight, packed in pouches that are foil-lined to keep in the humidity. If you see them in the store, it's possible to mistake them for packages of chewing tobacco. I have. Each variety of Backwoods–Regular, Sweet Aromatic (vanilla flavored), and Black 'N' Sweet Aromatic (vanilla and licorice flavored), all measuring 4⅛ x 27–are what's called "wild," meaning the ends of the cigars are ragged and uncut, in imitation of the old-fashioned, hand-rolled cheroots that legendary folks like Huckleberry Finn must have enjoyed. Just like Huck, Backwoods are not what you'd call fancy–they're made without a binder leaf.

Another variety is the DeNobili, a dark, Italian-type, popular American-made cheroot, and Dutch Masters offers a menthol cigarillo.

Guide to cigars by flavor

Some smokers like to pick and choose their cigars by size, and some like to do it by flavor, but I find that it helps to combine the two criteria and experiment with mixing and matching. That's why I've created this next section to complement the information just given on cigar sizes. I've divided cigars by their wrapper color so you can get an idea of the different flavors that are out there and, if you wish, you can do a little cross-referencing with the size categories to narrow your search to the cigars that you want to try.

Or maybe you just want to smoke them all!

Keep in mind that the wrapper leaf is responsible for 70 percent of a cigar's taste–think of it as the icing on a slice of cake. And just as different sizes provide different flavors–the rule of thumb being that the wider the ring gauge, the more powerfully flavored the cigar–different-color wrappers will provide clues as to how a cigar will taste. The lighter colors generally deliver a lighter flavor. Some smokers with a wide range of preferences find the mellow wrappers preferable at certain times of the day and the heavier, darker-colored wrappers better at others.

Again, I'd like to reiterate that I've assiduously avoided ranking a certain cigar as better or worse than another. I think that practice is silly. Cigar enjoyment is such an intensely personal experience that I'd be lying if I tried to tell you that what was the best cigar for me was also the best cigar for you. If that would indeed turn out to be the case, it would be more of a matter of coincidence than the cigar being an objectively "better" smoke.

If the filler leaves are the meat, the wrapper is the spice.

I've also purposely avoided shopworn descriptions like "nutty," "woody," and "coffeelike." These terms are more appropriately used by squirrels, carpenters, and Starbucks than by cigar smokers. Rather, I've classified the different cigars according to their expected strength of flavor. I think this is much more realistic and more objective. If I wanted to put something in my mouth that tasted like coffee, I certainly wouldn't light up a cigar!

Finally, I've also grouped the cigars under each category according to whether they're mostly handmade or machine-made. In the case of machine-bunched, hand-rolled cigars, I've placed them in the handmade category. The cigars I refer to as machine-made are the mass-marketed

---

80% of a cigar's flavor is determined by the wrapper.

varieties you'll find in most drug stores, convenience stores, and supermarkets. Again, though the premium and mass-market varieties are juxtaposed closely in the following paragraphs, keep in mind that there's a wide difference in the quality of their manufacture. And when appropriate, I've made reference to the cigar's construction, though the vast majority of cigars on the market today possess a perfectly suitable structure.

Double claro

Some people call these greenish wrappers "candela" or "claro claro." Double-claro cigars were so popular in the United States in the 1940s and into the 1960s that cigar-industry insiders tagged them with yet another name: "American Market Selection." Macanudo, the top-selling imported cigar in the United States, calls their double-claro brand a "jade." The vicissitudes of marketplace fashion have not been kind to the double claro, and it's much less popular among smokers today. The unusual color is attained by picking the wrapper leaf before it reaches full maturity and drying it quickly, so some double-claro leaves have a slightly bitter taste and an aroma on the acrid side, though most smokers would say that its flavor is very, very light.

Generally speaking, cigars with double-claro wrappers can be smoked anytime during the day; I would recommend them for daylight hours because of their relatively gentle flavor and aroma, though some brands, like the Hoyo de Monterrey varieties, tend to possess more tang. Double claros go well with a light lunch, a lager beer or mixed drinks like a martini or a margarita, or salty snacks.

Here are some of the handmade cigars available in this color.

■ Bering: Handmade in Honduras, Bering offers the Casino (7⅛ x 42), which is packaged in an aluminum tube; the Corona Grande (6¼ x 46); and the Plaza (6 x 43). All three have a smooth draw, mellow Honduran wrapper, and Cuban-seed filler. Look for the Bering varieties with the red bands.

■ **Don Diego:** The mild Don Diegos are handmade in the Dominican Republic by Consolidated Cigar. The brand offers three sizes of the candela wrapper grown in Connecticut.

■ **Hoyo de Monterrey:** Some of the fullest-bodied double claros on the market, the entire Hoyo de Monterrey line of twenty-one cigars, handmade in Honduras, is available in three wrapper colors: double claro, colorado claro, and maduro. They are all of excellent construction and made with an assortment of filler, mixed from Dominican, Honduran, and Nicaraguan tobaccos. If you're ever going to smoke a double claro after dinner, this is the one to try.

■ **Macanudo:** The famous "jade" cigars possess the Connecticut shade-grown wrapper and a Dominican-Mexican filler. These Macanudos are unique, and in their well-made uniqueness they're the epitome of the smooth and mild double-claro cigar. They're best enjoyed after a light midday meal or, if you get a chance, in the late morning.

Macanudo, which means "the greatest," or "copasetic" in colloquial Spanish, was founded in Jamaica in 1868 and today ranks as the most popular premium brand in the United States. The patriarch of the current Macanudo brand is Ramón Cifuentes, who revamped and reinvigorated the line at the behest of its owner, General Cigar, which established a satellite Macanudo factory in the Dominican Republic. Another cigar expert, Benjamin Menendez, carries on the brand's great tradition. The Dominican Macanudos are indistinguishable from their Jamaican counterparts, however, as both use the same Dominican-Mexican filler mix and Connecticut shade-grown wrapper, which is offered in every shade of the wrapper spectrum, from a greenish double claro (which Macanudo calls its "jade" wrapper) to the chocolate-brown maduro.

■ **Petrus:** Handmade in Honduras, the Petrus No. II (6¼ x 44) features a spicy Honduran wrapper and Honduran binder and filler.

■ **Pléiades:** A very mild cigar, the Centaurus (5¾ x 42) is the only cigar in the Dominican Republic's well-respected Pléiades line that features the double-claro Connecticut-grown wrapper.

■ **Punch:** Some Punch varieties I've heard described as cigars you don't want to finish, they're so good. I'd have to agree; they're fun to smoke. The Honduran firm offers twenty varieties of double-claro cigars, all made with Cuban-seed tobaccos.

When I see double-claro machine-made cigars, I'm reminded of the glory days of the candela wrapper, back when one could go over to the racetrack or the ballpark and find dozens of men smoking the greenish cigars. There's a certain nostalgia in that. Today, smoking is prohibited at many stadiums and the folks at the track—both men and women—are smoking the darker wrappers. Times are without a doubt better now. I can pick up the Yankees or the Mets—or the Braves and Cubs, for that matter—on cable and enjoy a cigar in the comfort of my own living room, and folks at the track, well, they ought to try a double claro some time, just to see what it's like.

Generally, mass-market brands that are available in the double-claro wrapper are very light-flavored. Here are some:

■ **As You Like It:** The following are not lottery-play suggestions, but varieties of the American-made Swisher International brand As You Like It available in the double-claro wrapper: No. 18 (6 x 41), No. 22 (4½ x 41), and No. 32 (6 x 43).

■ **Bances:** Made in Tampa by Villazon, the firm that owns Hoyo de Monterrey and Punch, Bances offers four cigars in the double-claro wrapper.

■ **Garcia y Vega:** The prototype of the double claro is Garcia y Vega's Gran Corona (6⅛ x 41), a mild, slightly bitter cigar that comes in a plastic tube. Open the tube and you'll find a Long Corona that's almost turtle green in color. Try it, you may like it. Other Garcia y Vega double claros include the Senator (4½ x 41) and the Elegante (6⅜ x 34), which are a bit less green but just as mild. By the way, though the binder is homogenized, the wrapper is natural.

Claro

It is not surprising that claro cigars were originally known in the U.S. as "clear" since claro means "clear" in spanish. Claro wrappers have been described as pale ginger, café au lait, beige, and wheat. Claros have also been nicknamed "natural wrappers" because somebody figured that claro and colorado claro, which is also sometimes called natural, were what wrappers were supposed to look like. This isn't necessarily so, but if you enjoy the smooth, mild flavor that claros often provide, perhaps you too will begin thinking that claro wrappers are the standard for what's "natural."

Like the double claro, cigars with claro wrappers are good daytime cigars, though some of them hold up nicely in the evening as long as you've eaten a light dinner that didn't make too many demands on your taste buds.

How to Tell a Real Cuban Cigar from a Counterfeit

There's a very significant black market for Cuban cigars in the United States, operated by unscrupulous people who are out to fatten their wallets by feeding the egos of American cigar smokers who want to impress people by offering Havanas around. The biggest appeal of the Cuban cigar is the romance; American smokers who are accustomed to the mellower Dominican or Honduran brands will probably find that Cuban cigars don't taste very good. Cuban tobacco is aged hardly at all, generally making the journey from farm to cigar box in seven months. I think the other Honduran and Caribbean blends, which are aged anywhere from three to five years, are superior to the Cuban; an estimated five million Cuban cigars are sold illegally every year in the United States.

When the U.S. trade embargo on Cuban products is finally lifted, I'm sure there will be a flurry of sales of Cuban cigars in this country, due mostly to curiosity. There's nothing that arouses interest in a product more than its prohibition! But I think that spike will settle down, and the other brands, which have established themselves in the American market, will again become dominant.

Until then, the possession and importation into the United States of Cuban cigars remains illegal, and U.S. cigar manufacturers and wholesalers have stood unanimously behind their country's policy. The people who do a business in the black marketing of these products do their country a disservice. Simply put, it's unpatriotic. But because Americans have so little exposure to Cuban cigars, I think it's helpful to consider some of the tricks that could be pulled by deceitful salespeople trying to foist fake Havanas on unsuspecting smokers.

First of all, all Cuban cigar boxes are sealed with a green-and-white stamp that reads: "Cuban government's warranty for cigars exported from Havana. Republica de Cuba. Sello de grantia nacional de procedencia." I've heard that these stamps can be easily duplicated, so just because the box has this stamp doesn't mean it's the real item. Boxes of prerevolutionary cigars have a stamp that reads, "Made In Havana-Cuba."

Is the box sealed? Have the bands been taken off the cigars? These are signs that perhaps the contents aren't the same as what's being advertised. Check out the color of the cigars in the box. If they are all the same color, chances are that you have a counterfeit on your hands. Boxes of Cuban cigars are notoriously inconsistent in color.

But the best test is to smoke one. Do you feel a burn in your chest? If you do, it's genuine. Cuban tobacco is a bit raw, having been rushed from the field to the cigar factory, resulting in a high ammonia content and a harsh, chest-stinging sensation when you puff on them.

If you're traveling out of the country, go ahead, satisfy your curiosity and sample a Cuban cigar, but beware: They are a disappointment to many people.

You'll find other stamps on the boxes of legitimate Cuban cigars, indicating where the cigars were made:

- BM: Briones Montoto, formerly Romeo y Julieta
- EL: El Laguito, the Cohiba factory
- FPG: Francisco Perez German, formerly Partagas
- FR: Fernando Roig, formerly La Corona
- JM: José Martí, formerly H. Upmann

If you ever make it down to Cuba, I advise you to buy your cigars from the many tourist shops, and not from a freewheeling street vendor. Counterfeits and items that "fell off the back of the truck" are rife on the street. The tourist shops take U.S. dollars, and the cigars are usually even less expensive there than in the duty-free shops. But keep in mind that Cuban officials will only allow you to leave the country with a maximum of $1,000 worth of cigars. So save your receipts. U.S. residents on an officially licensed visit to Cuba may legally return to the United States with up to $100 worth of cigars. But if you try to bring them in from Canada or Mexico or any other third country, you're violating the law and can be fined up to $50,000. That's an expensive cigar!

Better, I think, to count on it as an apéritif cigar, an accompaniment to cocktails and hors d'oeuvres before dinner rather than after. Claro cigars would complement a Chardonnay or a Zinfandel, and some of the fuller-bodied claros would stand up well to a Champagne. Or try a claro during a break from your workday; often the smooth mellowness will refresh you, and after smoking one you'll be able to dive back into your labors rejuvenated.

Here's a sampling of handmade cigars with a claro wrapper you could try.

- **Dunhill:** Aged for three months in cedar, Dunhill cigars are celebrated for their beautiful claro wrappers of Connecticut shade-grown tobacco. Made with Cuban-seed filler grown in the Dominican Republic, where it's completely handmade, the Dunhill line claims enthusiastic fans all over the world. Their fame began a century ago, when Dunhill became one of Britain's leading tobacconists. Today, Dunhill stores around the globe have branched out into lines of clothing, accessories, and luggage.

No less than seven of Dunhill's Dominican-made cigars are wrapped in claro Connecticut wrappers. The construction of each variety is superb and the flavor mild. These are elegant cigars.

- **J.R. Ultimate:** J.R. Tobacco's "Havana-style" cigar line includes four large cigars with a claro wrapper—Cetro (7 x 42), Corona (5⅝ x 45), No. 5 (6⅛ x 44), and Toro (6 x 50).

- **La Hoja Selecta:** Originally made in Cuba but now moved to Florida, La Hoja Selecta's entire line is made with Connecticut shade-grown claro wrapper leaves. These are very mild cigars.

- **La Plata:** The Los Angeles-based cigar maker offers five types in claro from its Premium series, including its Pyramid Classic (7 x 50), which, though a very big cigar, is not, alas, a Pyramid in shape.

- **Macanudo:** The well-made Jamaican cigar maker offers most of its catalog in a claro wrapper, from a cigarillo to a Double Corona, and even a Torpedo, nicknamed the Duke of Windsor. They possess a silky finish and a unique, mild flavor.

- **Santa Damiana:** This exceptional Dominican brand makes five claro cigars with a superior construction and exquisite appearance. They are all on the big side, from a Double Corona to a Corona Extra, with a Robusto, a Churchill, and a Lonsdale filling out its lineup.

Here are some machine-made varieties.

■ **J.R. Famous:** Available only through mail order and the chain of J.R. Tobacco stores, the J.R. Famous offers all four of its machine-made selections in a claro wrapper.

■ **Muniemaker:** One of the oldest U.S. cigar companies in continuous production, Muniemaker still occupies the same building in which it was founded in 1916 in New Haven, Connecticut. Their large cigars—Corona and Corona Extra—are available in a claro wrapper.

■ **Roi-Tan:** Machine-made in Puerto Rico by Consolidated Cigars with a homogenized binder and wrapper, the Roi-Tan line consists of a half dozen mass-market cigars, all featuring a light-colored wrapper. This solid mild cigar might be a good fit for someone who's curious about cigars but has never smoked one before.

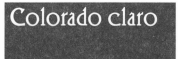
Colorado claro

"Colorado claro" is something of a misnomer. In Spanish, it means "clear red," but although some colorado claros have a hint of a reddish tinge, you'd never mistake them for, say, a fire engine. Rather, it's a shade darker than a claro, a tawny brown, and it makes for the most popular wrapper color among smokers throughout the world.

A well-made, properly cured colorado-claro cigar will have a silky, buttery look to it and a smooth, polished flavor. We're still in a mild-flavored category, but colorado claro has a bit more guts than a claro or a double claro. Some of the best colorado-claro leaf in the world is grown in Connecticut, Honduras, and Mexico.

Like the lighter styles, colorado-claro wrappers go well with hors d'oeuvres, Champagne, and other pre-meal victuals, and, in addition, the increased body stands up well with an ale or even a malt liquor. If your dinner hasn't been too spicy or too heavy, a colorado claro after the meal would be just fine, though I'd prefer a heavier cigar for that time of the evening.

Since the colorado claro is more of a middle category, most cigar makers in the world today manufacture products with this wrapper color.

Here's a sampling of some handmade varieties.

■ **Ashton:** The Connecticut shade-grown wrappers of the Ashton colorado-claro collection taste almost sweet. They are of the highest quality construction, with Cuban-seed Dominican filler.

■ **Davidoff:** Zino Davidoff emigrated to Switzerland from Russia in 1911, learned the tobacco business from his father, Henri, and in the 1920s traveled extensively in Latin America, where he studied the cigar-making industry firsthand. Through exclusivity contracts with his Cuban contacts, Davidoff sold and popularized Havana cigars throughout Europe upon his return to Switzerland, creating his own line after the Second World War and having a cigar named after him in 1969. Davidoff died at the age of 87 in 1994.

Generally speaking, Davidoff cigars are mellow and full-bodied, both at the same time. The entire line is made with a Connecticut colorado-claro wrapper, Dominican binder, and Cuban-seed Dominican filler.

■ **Montecristo:** The Cuban counterpart of this brand name is famous, and it wasn't until a short time ago that Consolidated Cigar brought out a Dominican-made cigar with the Montecristo label. The outstanding characteristic of these cigars is the aftertaste. Montecristo's six varieties are all smooth and mild, yet their taste lingers on the palate. This is a very sophisticated smoke.

■ **Nat Sherman:** The Exchange Selection—named after New York City's better-known telephone exchanges in the days before faxes and modems—offers five smooth varieties, the Academy No. 2 (5 x 31), Murray Hill No. 7 (6 x 38), Butterfield No. 8 (6½ x 42), Trafalgar No. 4 (6 x 47), and Oxford No. 5 (7 x 49).

The Gotham Selection—named after the four locations of the Nat Sherman store in Manhattan—include No. 65 (6 x 32), No. 1400 (6¼ x 44), No. 711 (6 x 50), and No. 500 (7 x 50) and come in a handsome, curve-sided leather box.

The Nat Sherman V.I.P. Selection is named after some of New York's most famous people. The Zigfeld (6¾ x 38) is a fancytail. The three other varieties are the Morgan (7 x 42), the Astor (4½ x 50), and the Carnegie (6 x 48). The V.I.P.s are made in the Dominican Republic with Connecticut wrappers and a mix of Brazilian and Dominican filler tobaccos.

■ **Paul Garmirian:** Sold since 1991, Paul Garmirian cigars have already made their mark on the international market. They have a pleasant aroma and are subtle, yet possess a bite. P.G. offers more than a dozen varieties, from a Giant to a Short Panatela.

■ **Romeo y Julieta Vintage:** When the U.S. government finally lifts the Cuban embargo, one of the companies that will probably be embroiled in some convoluted international legal brouhahas will be Romeo y Julieta. The name is famous for its Cuban brand of cigars, and after Castro's rise to power, three Romeo y Julieta brands were churning out cigars for the world's smokers. Now there are only two—in Cuba and in the Dominican Republic—but it'll be a mess sorting out the proprietorships for this and other expatriate cigar manufacturers.

> ## "Hand-rolled" means the cigar was machine-bunched before a human roller "finished" it. These cigars can be every bit as satisfying as the more expensive "handmade" varieties.

All this has very little to do with the Romeo y Julieta Vintage series, which features an almost oily Connecticut wrapper and smoothly blended Dominican filler. I would recommend smoking this cigar without accompaniment. Its taste is fragile and mild, but immensely satisfying.

■ **Temple Hall:** Named after a Jamaican tobacco plantation, Temple Hall was founded in 1876 and recently reintroduced by its current owner, General Cigar. Handmade in Jamaica from Connecticut wrapper and a mix of Jamaican, Dominican, and Mexican filler, Temple Hall would be a good smoke for the enthusiast who's ready to graduate from the mass-market varieties to a handmade cigar.

■ **V Centennial:** This handsome cigar is a newcomer on the scene, introduced in late 1993, but it has proved very popular and is found in many fine tobacco shops. The mildness of its Connecticut wrapper is offset by its full-bodied blend of filler tobaccos, making it one of the more robust colorado-claro cigar lines.

There is a good selection of machine-made cigars:

■ **Antonio y Cleopatra:** Puerto Rico-made A & C, as it's called, is one of the industry standbys. Its four-cigar Grenadiers series (Grenadiers, 6¼ x 33½; Grenadiers Miniatures, 4½ x 28; Grenadiers Panatelas, 5⅜ x 35; and Grenadiers Presidentes, 5⅝ x 42) is short-filled, with a homogenized binder, and is graced with a Connecticut shade-grown wrapper. This cigar is highly recommended for the beginner, or for someone who wants a no-nonsense mellow smoke, or for folks on a budget.

- **El Producto:** El Producto is machine-made in Puerto Rico by Consolidated Cigars using homogenized filler and binder. The entire line has colorado-claro wrappers, and it's one of the most consistent brand names on the market today.

- **Hav-A-Tampa:** To the delight of their many rabid devotees, Hav-A-Tampas are churned out by the thousands using full automation. Their built-in wooden tips make them distinctive and very popular.

"Gentlemen, you may smoke."

- **King Edward:** Perhaps the No. 1-selling brand in the world, King Edward is made by Swisher International in its automated plant in Georgia. King Edwards, made with a homogenized binder, are one of the few "dusted" cigars on the market. That means that after they're assembled, a fine tobacco dust is sprayed on them to mask any imperfections in the wrapper. Some of their cigars also feature a wooden tip.

- **Muriel:** One of the reigning royalty of the world's mass-produced cigars, Muriel, made in Puerto Rico, has a dozen or so very popular mild selections to choose from.

- **White Owl:** General Cigar's top seller, the White Owl line consists of nine cigars, all made with homogenized binder and mild wrapper.

Colorado

Whether by the vagaries of the system of classification or because it's kind of an in-between color, cigars that tout themselves as possessing colorado wrappers are less prevalent in the marketplace today than any of the others. I know for sure that some colorado claro wrappers and colorado maduro could easily be categorized as colorado, but they aren't.

This is not a problem for the curious smoker. As you and your lighter travel the spectrum from double claro to maduro, you'll find some very satisfying varieties in the colorado grouping.

Colorado wrappers, once so popular in Britain that they're nicknamed "English Market Selection," are cured thoroughly and aged a bit longer than the lighter wrapper leaves, and consequently they possess more body.

If you're going to smoke outside, for example while shooting a round of golf, you'll want a cigar that can stand up to the wind and the distracting elements of the weather. A colorado wrapper might be a good idea if you desire a smoke that's still on the milder side.

Colorado wrappers might also be a welcome addition late in the afternoon or early evening, when you've finished your work for the day and want to treat yourself to a smoke before dinner, but don't want to overpower your mouth and ruin your enjoyment of the meal.

Here are some handmade cigars to look for.

- **Avo:** Avo Uzevian, the originator of the Avo line, is one of the true characters of the cigar industry. Born in Beirut, Lebanon, Uzevian was trained as a pianist at New York's famous Juilliard School and was reportedly once the official pianist to the Pahlevis, the ruling family of Iran until the Ayatollah came to power. He even won a measure of fame as composer of Frank Sinatra's "Strangers in the Night." As a U.S. soldier, he fell in love with cigars, and in 1986 he started his own brand of Dominican-made cigars. The entire line is composed of cigars with colorado Connecticut shade-grown wrappers and is renowned for its richness, combined with a mellowness. The XO series of three cigars–the Preludio (6 x 40), the Intermezzo (5½ x 50), and the Maestoso (7 x 48)–seem to be instructions from their maestro on when to smoke them.

- **Fonseca:** One of the finest cigars on the market today, the Dominican-made Fonseca combines a Connecticut wrapper with filler tobacco grown in the Dominican Republic's famous Cibao Valley for a medium-bodied smoke. If you're interested in exotic sizes, try the Triangular (5½ x 56), which is a cone-shaped Pyramid.

- **Juan Clemente:** This Dominican brand, launched in the United States in 1985, offers an entire line of colorado wrappers, including its Club Selection series, which is aged four years before it's sold. These include No. 1 (6 x 50), No. 2 (4½ x 46), No. 3 (7 x 44), and No. 4 (5¾ x 42). Because the Juan Clemente factory is the only large cigar manufacturing center not located in the Dominican duty-free zone, it can sell its wares to tourists who visit. This is handy for the marketing department, because Juan Clemente only makes four hundred fifty thousand cigars per year–a small number relative to the rest of the industry. In addition, the maverick cigar maker packs his boxes with twenty-four cigars. Everybody else packs twenty-five.

You may want to try a machine-made colorado.

■ **Zino:** The mass-market portion of the Davidoff legacy makes a half dozen varieties of colorado small cigars at its factories in Holland and Switzerland. The dry cigars' wrappers are grown in Sumatra. One of my favorite names for a cigar is the Relax Sumatra, a Slim Panatela manufactured in Switzerland.

Colorado maduro

Now we're getting into the spicier, fuller-bodied varieties of cigar wrapper, able to hold their own anytime you want to relax and unwind and spend a length of time with friends and your cigar. The colorado maduro is best after dinner, with a glass of cognac, sherry, or port, or over a cup of espresso. It does just fine with dessert, which would overpower a milder cigar. Though not as heavy or sweet in its way as a maduro, the colorado maduro is known for its depth, its robust aroma, its powerful flavor, and its lingering aftertaste.

My favorite colorado-maduro wrapper is grown in Cameroon, but, unfortunately, worldwide demand has far outstripped the supply of this fine wrapper, and the current shortage of choice Cameroon leaf has sent cigar makers looking elsewhere for appropriate colorado-maduro leaf. They've found it in Honduras and Mexico, where the San Andrés Valley is quickly becoming a mecca for those who, like me, enjoy Mexican tobacco despite its bad rap. Ecuador and Nicaragua have also filled the gap created by the shortage of Cameroon, and it's exciting to think that the next few years will see the growth of the tobacco industry in those two countries, which have already made their imprint on the international market and still possess a great deal of potential.

Short-filled cigars have bits of chopped tobacco inside. Long-filled cigars have whole leaves.

Maduro means "ripe" or "mature" in Spanish, and the colorado-maduro wrapper has the brown tinting of a fully aged tobacco leaf. I've heard it described as a milk-chocolate color, but it's usually a shade or two lighter than that.

Colorado-maduro wrapper is made of tobacco from all over the world. Here are a few examples of handmade cigars made with the colorado-maduro leaf, with every effort made to show you the diverse origins of this aromatic wrapper.

■ **Bauzá:** Bauzá's entire line of nine handmade Dominican cigars is made with a Cameroon wrapper and Dominican filler and binder. They are extremely well-made and provide a medium-bodied smoke. They also have sizes to please everyone, from a panatela to a Double Corona.

■ **El Rey del Mundo:** Made with a Sumatra-seed wrapper grown in Ecuador with Honduran filler, El Rey del Mundo, "king of the world" in Spanish, is the brainchild of Lew Rothman of J.R. Tobacco. It's spicy and strong, has a lot of backbone, and is available by mail order in a wide range of sizes. Highlights include the Double Corona (7 x 49) and a Torpedo called Flor de Llaneza, named after Frank Llaneza, a longtime tobacco man and one of the most revered cigar blenders of all time. The man is a visionary, and the cigar does him an honor.

■ **Nat Sherman:** The Manhattan, Host, and Landmark selections all feature colorado-maduro wrappers.

Named after the city's famous neighborhoods, the Manhattan Selection of five cigars features a spicy Mexican wrapper and a delicate aftertaste. The sizes are Beekman (5¼ x 28), Tribeca (6 x 31), Chelsea (6½ x 38), Gramercy (6¾ x 43), and Sutton (5½ x 49).

The Host Selection includes the Hudson (6 x 34), the Hamilton (5½ x 42), Hunter (6¾ x 43), Harrington (5 x 47), Hobart (7½ x 49), and Hampton (7 x 50).

The five Landmark Selection cigars are named after locations every cabdriver in New York City should know—just hop into the cab and ask for them by name. They have a Cameroon wrapper and a fuller, more robust flavor. They include the Metropole (6 x 34), the Hampshire (5½ x 42), the Algonquin (6¾ x 43), the Vanderbilt (5 x 47), and the Dakota (7½ x 49). I often recommend Landmark Selection cigars as an accompaniment to dessert and brandy after dinner.

Each of the Nat Sherman cigars features a band with a picture of the clock that sits above our Fifth Avenue store in Manhattan and a different color background denoting each selection. They're available via mail order.

- **Partagas:** Made famous by Ramón Cifuentes and now run by General Cigar in the Dominican Republic, Partagas features Cameroon wrappers and a mixture of Dominican and Mexican fillers. Especially rare are the Limited Reserve series and the 150th Anniversary Signature series, which came out in late 1995. If you can get your hands on one of those, try it. If you don't like it, send the rest of the box to me!

- **Ramón Allones:** A heavier cigar, made with a Cameroon wrapper, the Dominican-made, General Cigar-owned Ramón Allones line–not to be confused with the Cuban–consists of six varieties of cigar, all featuring a colorado-maduro wrapper.

  - **Royal Jamaica:** Despite the name, Royal Jamaica cigars are handmade in the Dominican Republic. Their rich, aromatic wrappers are made from Sumatran leaf, and the filler is an old family recipe that includes the same Jamaican tobacco that was originally used in its cigars when the factory was located in Jamaica–before Hurricane Hugo's swath of destruction leveled the plant in 1989. The factory will be moving back to Jamaica.

  - **Te-Amo:** Beloved in some quarters, dismissed in others, Te-Amo was at one time one of the New York area's most popular brands. The cigar, with about two dozen varieties–including maduro and colorado-claro wrappers as well–is made with all-Mexican tobacco from the celebrated San Andrés Valley. The darker wrappers are medium-bodied, make for a good casual, everyday smoke, and are mild enough for the middle of the day. Te-Amo also makes a short-filled cigar.

Don't be alarmed by the stamp that reads "contains non-tobacco products." It refers to a small amount of cellulose vegetable paste in homogenized binder that's odorless and tasteless.

- **H. Upmann:** Since 1844, the H. Upmann name has been known around the world. Its entire handmade Dominican line, now overseen by Consolidated Cigar, sports a colorado-maduro wrapper grown in Sumatra. You can tell the Cuban version from the Dominican by its band–the Cuban band reads "Havana" where the Dominican says "1844." If you're a more experienced smoker and are looking for a powerful smoke, try the wide-bodied H. Upmann Cabinet Selection, which features the Columbo (8 x

50), the Corsario (5½ x 50), and the Robusto (4¾ x 50). They're sold in boxes of fifty.

The colorado-maduro wrapper is featured in the following mass-market brands.

■ **Dutch Masters:** A spicier machine-made cigar, Dutch Masters offers a half-dozen varieties of short-filled product with homogenized binder, some of them available in menthol. Now made by Consolidated Cigar, Dutch Masters was a lot of people's first cigar experience.

■ **Erik:** Erik is ubiquitous in stores throughout the United States. It features three varieties of cigarillos–Natural, Menthol, and Cherry Flavor–all with a filter tip.

■ **Havana Blend:** This American machine-made cigar claims to use stockpiled pre-Castro Cuban tobacco in its seven varieties.

Maduro

Because it would be outrageously expensive to grow maduro tobacco in the field, all the maduro now on the market is made from the ripest leaves that have been either steamed or boiled until they're the dark brown color that makes a maduro cigar. If the leaves were to be kept on the plants for as long as is needed to yield the rich coffee color, your cigar might cost as much as twenty or thirty dollars! Since there's no significant variation in flavor using the shortcut, cigar makers have spared smokers the additional expense.

Maduro is the darkest-colored wrapper tobacco currently on the market. Most smokers I talk to have only seen pictures of oscuro cigars in books and have never smoked a cigar that was called an oscuro (which means "dark" in Spanish). I suspect that industry standard makers simply lump all very dark cigars into the maduro category these days.

Maduro cigars are rich and full-bodied, though not as aromatic as some of the lighter shades. I call them the perfect dessert cigars, because their richness is best enjoyed after a big meal. Light up a maduro and pass me a piece of chocolate cake, and I'll be very happy.

Though maduros are popular enough today, they're considered a little off-beat. But there was a time when they were thought of as the standard Cuban wrapper color, and they were exported to Europe by the millions in a day and age when that was still a huge number. Hence they've acquired the nickname "Spanish Market Selection."

Some smokers actually find some maduro brands mellower than their colorado-maduro counterparts, and that's to be expected from a wrapper leaf that's been subjected to the cooking recipes of the individual cigar makers. So if you're expecting a deep, powerful, robust flavor from every maduro you try, you'll be surprised. The strength varies from brand to brand—and sometimes from cigar to cigar.

Here are some handmade brands.

■ **Arturo Fuente:** One of the most respected names in the business, Arturo Fuente blends as many as four different tobaccos into its cigars, and each selection features a different blend, so taste, body, and aroma vary according to cigar type. Most of their two dozen selections are offered in a maduro wrapper.

■ **Cuesta-Rey:** The first cigar maker in the United States to use cellophane packaging, Cuesta-Rey was founded in 1884 by Angel La Madrid Cuesta, who brought on a partner named Peregrino Rey. They established a factory in Ybor City during its heady days of world cigar leadership; then in 1986 they moved their hand-rolling operations to the Dominican Republic, maintaining their factory in Tampa for their machine-made cigars.

Cuesta-Rey uses a Connecticut shade-grown wrapper for its cigars, which come under two subheadings, the Cabinet Selection and the Centennial Selection. The Cabinet Selection is somewhat milder, and the Centennial Selection is aged an additional month before shipping. Both selections have a wide variety of sizes in a maduro wrapper.

■ **Excalibur:** A meaty cigar made in Honduras by Hoyo de Monterrey, the Excaliburs wear a band similar to the Hoyos, but the word "Excalibur" is printed on the bottom. Seven varieties are available in a wide range of sizes. These cigars are on the mellow side for maduros, but still go great with coffee and dessert.

■ **Henry Clay:** Named after the nineteenth-century American statesman, who maintained Cuban business interests, and originally made in Cuba, Henry Clay is now run by Consolidated Cigar in the Dominican Republic. They come in three varieties, all maduro: Breva (5½ x 42), Breva a la Conserva (5⅝ x 46), and Breva Fina (6⅛ x 48). An idealized rendering of the Cuban factory still adorns the inside of the Henry Clay box.

■ **La Finca:** This brand gives a strong indication that Nicaraguan tobacco is back after a long hiatus due to political unrest. Made entirely of Nicaraguan tobacco from the Jamastran Valley, there are nine cigar selections, all of them available in colorado-maduro or maduro wrappers. La Finca, which means "estate" in Spanish, is distributed by J.R. Tobacco and has a reputation for being full-bodied and robust.

■ **Licenciados:** If you're looking for big cigars with flavor that's strong but doesn't overwhelm, you may find it here. Licenciados is handmade in the Dominican Republic with Connecticut wrapper and Dominican filler. Its No. 200 (5¾ x 42), No. 300 (6¾ x 42), No. 400 (6 x 50), and No. 500 (8 x 50) can all give possibly more than an hour of smoking apiece.

■ **Nat Sherman:** Nat Sherman's maduro cigars are included in the City Desk Selection, named in memory of New York's bygone heyday of daily newspapers. They are the Gazette (6 x 42), Dispatch (6½ x 46), Telegraph (6 x 50), and Tribune (7½ x 50).

Some machine-made varieties are available in the maduro wrapper.

■ **Topstone:** Machine-made with long filler and a real tobacco binder in Tampa by Villazon, a company owned in part by Frank Llaneza, one of this century's top tobacco men, Topstone offers a Natural Dark series that includes a Churchill (called the Executive) and a panatela, both made from Connecticut maduro leaf.

■ **Travis Club:** Travis Club offers seven varieties of long-filled, 100-percent-tobacco machine-made cigars available in maduro and colorado claro.

Chapter Four

Humidors and Accessories: The Care and Smoking of Your Cigar

A premium cigar is like a living, breathing thing, and it needs to be cared for properly from the time you purchase it to the time you smoke it. As soon as you buy the cigar and take it out of the tobacconist's humidor, the clock starts ticking. The responsibility for protecting it falls to you, the smoker. Don't let a fine cigar dehydrate! Store it promptly and properly. The cigar's tobacco can lose its moisture very quickly, and once that happens, its flavor ebbs and dies, and a lot of the pleasure of smoking is lost too.

Most smokers don't realize just how fast a cigar can be sapped of its freshness. In dry or cold conditions, it may only take a matter of hours. Though you can often bring the life back to cigars that have dried out, it's better to keep them in good smoking condition at all times. That way you won't have to go to the extra trouble of resuscitating them, which is difficult to do, and they'll always be ready to smoke. Keeping them properly humidified will also lessen the possibility of breakage or loss.

A sense of humidors

Cigars thrive when the temperature is between 68 and 72 degrees Fahrenheit and the humidity is between 68 and 72 percent, with 70 percent humidity/70 degrees being the average. When you buy a cigar from a reputable tobacconist, the merchant will have kept the cigar in a humidor—a cabinet, box, or even an entire room where the temperature and humidity are controlled—and the minute the cigar leaves that controlled climate for a drier one, it begins to dehydrate. Of course, if you live in the swamps of Georgia, you may need a humidor to keep your cigars from becoming too moist and swelling up! Regardless, maintaining the condition of your cigars at home or at work is essential to smoking pleasure. It's not as complicated as it may sound. I'll show you how to make your own humidor, what to look for if you want to buy one, how to keep the humidor functioning well, and how to protect your cigars outside the controlled environment.

A cigar can turn from world class to dry and unsmokable within a matter of hours.

Humidors can be as elaborate as a finely crafted polished wood cabinet that holds a thousand cigars or as simple as a plastic bag. The most common variety is the desktop box, equipped with a humidification apparatus and a hygrometer, a device that measures the relative humidity inside. Surprisingly, a plastic bag can work just as well as an expensive cabinet humidor in keeping your cigars in top smoking condition.

These classic desktop humidors are made of wood and feature eight layers of hand-rubbed lacquer. The trays are made of Spanish cedar and are woven to allow the humidity to travel evenly through the layers. Note the round humidification device, on the inside of the lid, and the small hygrometer, to keep track of the humidity.

Of course, some people smoke dry cigars and love them, and Europe as a whole has preferred the dry, short-filled cigar to the moist, premium-quality smoke since the days of Dutch colonialism in America and Indonesia. But the vast majority of smokers in the Western Hemisphere—and premium cigar lovers the world over—have gone to great trouble, time, and expense to keep their cigars moist and flavorful as long as the technology has existed to do so. And remember that it was an Englishman—Alfred Dunhill—who first popularized the humidor, installing one in his London shop back in 1907.

Making your own

If you're just starting out, or if you smoke cigars only occasionally, you can make your own "dormitory humidor." It's the simplest method around, and since it's made of things most people keep around the house, the cost is negligible. I call it a dormitory humidor because it's a lot of people's first humidor and it can be assembled anywhere.

Take one of those airtight, hard plastic containers that are normally used for storing leftover food and put a shot glass or some other low glass inside it. Place a piece of clean sponge in the glass and fill the glass with distilled water, soaking the sponge. (There's nothing magical about distilled water, but tap water contains minerals, mainly calcium, that will clog your humidification equipment, and the chlorine in tap water will be absorbed by the cigars over time and alter their taste. Not good. So make the investment of a dollar for a gallon of distilled water, and it should last you a solid year.) Make sure there's room between the top of the glass and the top of the container in order for the moisture to circulate. If the cigars you've purchased are wrapped in cellophane, leave that on. Cellophane is not the evil a lot of people make it out to be. Sure, it inhibits enjoyment of the cigar's aroma somewhat, but it also acts as the cigar's shield against harmful elements in the environment. Place the cigars in the container. Then place the lid on the box. Replenish the water as needed. This device will protect your cigars from drying out and becoming stale. Even if you've just bought a couple of cigars to smoke later, or you've just received a gift and don't want to light up immediately, it's important to remember that a cigar is a delicate product. It needs to be kept in a controlled atmosphere that will preserve its flavor, bouquet, and aroma.

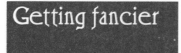

Getting fancier

If you're a more dedicated cigar smoker, a humidor is a valuable investment, or you can hint around at birthday time–they make great gifts! The fancier, manufactured humidors can run anywhere between $250 and $8,250. For $250, expect to get a leather- or wood-finished box with a 25-cigar capacity and perfectly good technology to monitor the humidity level of your stash. For $8,250, you can buy an expertly crafted mahogany cabinet with Spanish cedar interior, an electric fan to spread the humidity evenly throughout the hundreds of cigars you'll be able to store within, and a digital hygrometer to regulate the humidity. Besides providing protection for your beloved cigars, a humidor like this is also a beautiful piece of furniture.

The more you smoke, the more it'll pay off to purchase a humidor. First, your cigars will be ready to smoke anytime you want them. Second, you'll never "lose" a cigar if you keep your collection in a

Home Humidor Advantage

When the original Madison Square Garden in New York was retired, Nat Sherman was asked to create a cigar humidor from small sections of the floor of the old basketball court where Willis Reed led the New York Knicks to their first world championship in 1970. Holding 50 cigars and retailing for $1,250, the limited edition of 250 humidors is now a keepsake that combines a piece of the most famous arena in the world with one of life's greatest pleasures.

A Humidor of One's Own

If you're one of those people whose imagination cannot be corralled, why should you stop at a mere cabinet capable of holding a thousand cigars? Try adding an entire smoking room onto your house! Nat Sherman has helped to design many such units, from the size of a closet to a complete wing. This may sound too much like a commer-

cial, but the country's largest walk-in humidor is located in the Nat Sherman store on Fifth Avenue in Manhattan, where we have three million cigars preserved in top condition. We invite our customers to enjoy a smoke inside, on one of the humidor's leather lounge chairs.

Nothing in the world better stimulates a feeling of camaraderie than sharing cigars. Here, two customers enjoy a leisurely midday smoke in the walk-in humidor at the Nat Sherman store located at the corner of Fifth Avenue and 42nd Street.

If you live in the swamps of Georgia,
you may need a humidor to keep your cigars
from becoming too moist.

This cabinet humidor doubles as a piece of fine furniture. It's made of rubbed mahogany and all the fittings and hardware are solid marine brass. It boasts a microprocessor that activates an electric fan to keep all ten of its drawers—and up to 1,000 cigars—at the same humidity. Around the Nat Sherman store, we call this the "ultimate ultimate humidor."

regulated atmosphere; you'll know your investment is safe. There's no sense selecting and purchasing a premium quality product if you're not going to protect it. As my father used to say, "You don't buy a Duesenberg and then park it on the street." And third, the pleasure a cigar brings is magnified when it's selected from a beautiful humidor. The enjoyment of a cigar is a matter affecting all the senses. The cigars' bouquet, their aroma, the silky sheen or deep glow of their wrappers, the symmetry and evenness of their color—all of it is enhanced by the polished-wood or leather-finished humidor. Sure, the dormitory humidor is a practical way to keep your cigars, but if practicality was all that mattered in life, we'd all be driving Yugos.

Most manufactured humidors feature a small hygrometer to measure the ambient humidity in the box and a humidification device, which is usually a simple brass cage attached to the inside of the lid, filled with a substance called phenolic resin, known for retaining and spreading moisture without giving off an aroma. Sometimes humidor makers will use red clay instead of the resin, but this is becoming less and less common. Either way, this is the part of the humidor that gets the infusion of distilled water. The humidor should come with a device that resembles an eyedropper. Use the eyedropper to add water to the humidifying substance to keep your humidor functioning properly.

What kind of humidor should you buy? That choice is a personal one that only you can make with the assistance of a fine tobacconist. Look for a

**Take your pick:
mahogany or leather?**

Spanish cedar interior and quality workmanship—seamless closure, fluidity in the lid's opening and closing, finished joinery, ease in refilling the humidification system's water supply—and once you've established that the humidor is Spanish cedar and well made, the only difference between them is size and aesthetics. Most humidors come in three different sizes, accommodating 25, 50, and 100 cigars. Different kinds of wood are available. Beautiful hand-rubbed wood and lacquer finishes are very appealing, though I must say that I personally enjoy the antiqued leather humidors with their gold hand-tooling. Since the types of wood and leather don't affect the functioning of the humidor, my only advice is to choose a color that doesn't clash with the rest of the furnishings in the room.

If you're on the go, some tobacconists offer a humidor specifically manufactured for travelers. Some even sell briefcases with a special cigar compartment or a mini-humidor inside. Or you can carry your cigars in a plastic container with you, or you can preserve your cigars in a similar low-cost manner using a plastic bag. The kind that lock shut are best. Either way, just place a clean piece of damp sponge inside a secondary plastic bag in which you have punched numerous holes, and put that bag in with the cigars. Be careful that the sponge and the cigars can't touch—if they do, the cigars will leach the dampness out of the sponge and become moldy or swell up with the excess moisture. Even if the cigars are wrapped in cellophane, it's a good idea to protect the cigars by using the perforated-bag-in-the-bag trick.

If you're giving a box of cigars as a gift and they're going to be kept around the house for a while, it's a good idea to wrap up the box in an airtight plastic bag. It helps retain the moisture, which is essential to keeping the cigars fresh.

How humid the humidor?

Maybe you've purchased a cigar you bought in a candy store that didn't have a humidor, or you smoked a cigar you'd left in a desk drawer for a few days. You've tasted what a dry cigar can be like—disappointing and unpleasant, and altogether different from the enjoyment garnered from a properly conditioned cigar. Now that you appreciate a fine cigar in top shape and have either made the decision to invest in a manufactured humidor or assembled one of your own, you want to know how best to put it to use.

At the very least, a humidor should keep a cigar moist enough so that the wrapper doesn't become brittle and break. As I mentioned earlier, cigars are best kept in an environment that doesn't fluctuate outside of 68 to 72 degrees and 68 to 72 percent humidity. You'd be surprised at how much difference there is between those four degrees and percentage points of humidity, so if you have a hygrometer to measure humidity and a thermometer to measure temperature, start with the 70/70 midpoint and experiment within the 68/72 range. Make note of the moistness and aroma of the different settings or locations until you can tailor the cigars to the way you like them. Different people prefer different degrees of moisture. The European predilection, as I said before—influenced over time by the Dutch growers—tends toward the unhumidified cigar. Though the trend worldwide is toward the moist, premium style of cigar, a lot of Europeans still shun the use of humidors and smoke their cigars the old-fashioned way—dry.

Just as personal preferences vary, so do cigar types. Cigars are usually packed or bundled two different ways—the "13-top" and the "8-9-8." The "13-top" is the method used in the traditional cigar box, with 13 cigars on top and 12 on the bottom, with the row finished with a cedar block. These

70/70: 70 degrees and 70 percent humidity.

cigars are packed under pressure, and if you'll notice, they look slightly squared when you take them out of the box. They'll need to be kept in slightly higher humidity because they're constructed differently than the "8-9-8," which may use more tobacco. Try notching the humidity up a couple percentage points for the "13-top" cigars—say, to 72 percent—and working your way down if you want.

(Left) The 13-top box. It holds 13 cigars on the top row and 12 below. A piece of cedar usually fills out the lower row.

(Above) The 8-9-8 box. These are held together with a ribbon.

Your personal habits are a factor in determining the right humidity level for your private stock of cigars. Ask yourself some questions: How often do you open your humidor? When you open it, do you leave it open to enjoy the aroma, or do you close it right away? If you open it frequently or leave it open for a long period of time to let the scent waft through the air, obviously your humidity level will need to be slightly higher than the average—but only a percentage point or two. If you open the humidor only for a second or two each day, try setting your humidity at 68 and work up if you find your cigars too dry. Do you select cigars to smoke later in the day, or do you usually smoke them immediately? If you carry cigars around in your pocket, you might want to condition them with a higher humidity level to start with—say, 72 percent. Do you have air conditioning in the room? Air conditioning—as well as most heating systems—leaches moisture out of the air and creates a very dry environment. You'll need a slightly higher humidity than the average in your humidor if that's the case. Be sure to take all this into account.

Mesmerized by technology

What do you do if your humidor doesn't have a hygrometer or a thermometer to help you regulate the cigar's environment? Use your senses. It's easy to become mesmerized by the technology if you have it, and tempting to spend all sorts of time checking the meter and adjusting the humidor according to the numbers, but the truest indicator of the condition of your cigars—regardless of whether or not you have the technology—is how they feel, look, and smell. Open the box and touch them. Do they feel as moist as you'd like them to be? Do their wrappers bounce back to shape when you squeeze them? Smell them. Are you enticed by their aroma? Look at them. Do the veins of their wrappers look alive and inviting? Attuning yourself to the subtleties of the cigars' condition will increase your enjoyment of the cigar experience and help you maintain the cigar that's tailor-made to your tastes.

I like my cigars on the moist side, and I find that a humidity around 71 percent yields the best results for the kind of cigar I like to smoke.

If you're like me—a true cigar lover—and you enjoy smoking at work as well as at home, it's a good idea to purchase or make a humidor for the office, too. The forced-air environments of modern offices are real cigar killers. Without the benefit of a humidor, your cigars will probably start to crisp up and lose their flavor by the middle of the afternoon.

Since a cigar taken out of the humidor in the morning could turn dry and stale by noon, use a pocket cigar case to protect them from breakage and dehydration. Cases are available in leather or precious metals, and both work well. You can even reuse one of the metal tubes in which some cigars are sold. The case will not only protect the cigar from the inhospitable environment, it'll also prevent it from rubbing against your coat, a pen, or the other cigars, which can ruin a cigar in minutes. And, where possible, be sure to leave the cellophane on.

I'm often asked if it's okay to put two different cigars next to each other in the same humidor. Well, there is some marriage of aroma and flavor between the two, and over a long period of time they'll begin to smell and taste like each other. But over a short period of time, I really don't think you'll be able to detect a difference. If you're worried about this, many humidors already come equipped with cedar dividers, and slipping one between the two cigars should ease your mind. Or you can make your own divider by cutting a piece of cardboard or snapping off a piece of a cedar

Nat Sherman Cigar Myth No. 1

"Store your cigars in the refrigerator." This myth actually has a basis in sound advice. You might remember back when your mother or grandmother owned a refrigerator, and she had to defrost it every week or so because of the moisture buildup. That was before today's frost-free appliances, which sap the humidity out of the air and can kill your cigar faster than anything. At least those refrigerators didn't harm the moisture level of the cigars. But storing your cigar in the refrigerator will also cause it to absorb the odor of whatever food you have in there. If you store your cigars in one of today's refrigerators, they'll dry out quickly and end up tasting more like onions or Chinese take-out than fine tobacco. Back in the old days, the stronger-flavored cigars probably benefited from this, but today's premium brands are much improved and deserve to be savored without condiments.

Nat Sherman Cigar Myth No. 2

"Sliced apple stored with your cigars will keep them moist." Some apple farmer somewhere started this myth, and it worked for him, because he replaced the apple every few hours or so. But it won't work for you because, while quickly releasing its self-contained moisture into the tobacco—as well as its flavor—the apple also quickly creates mold, which will spread to the cigars and ruin them.

Nat Sherman Cigar Myth No. 3

"Cigar tobacco will continue to ferment in the humidor, and you should age your cigars a certain amount of time before you smoke them—as long as ten years." Some people swear by this advice, but who can stand not to smoke a perfectly good cigar for that length of time? Once the tobacco is in the cigar, it should have been aged and cured as much as it needs to be and it's pretty much been stabilized and equilibrated. So I say enjoy smoking your cigars—and don't bother waiting for them to become antiques.

Kept properly, a cigar can last forever.
Does that mean that the first Mayan stogies
may still be around?

---

cigar box and placing it between the two different cigars. If you own one of the larger humidors, by all means leave the cigars in the box they came in. That'll stop any intermarriage before it starts.

Stored properly, a cigar will stay fresh indefinitely. I say that because nobody has ever kept one so long that it's deteriorated. Theoretically, the first Mayan cigars may still be around—if someone was crafty enough to stick them in a humidor and keep the humidity level between 68 and 72 percent! We have some pre-Castro Havanas from 1956 in our New York warehouse that are still in perfect smoking condition. We occasionally give them to charity auctions to be used as fund raisers. Their cellophane wrappers have turned yellow, but the cigars are fine. I don't know of any cigars still around that have been manufactured any earlier than those.

Lifesavers

Humidors will maintain the freshness of your cigars, but they won't bring back a cigar that's become so dry and stale that you'd rather not smoke it. Instead of throwing the cigar away, which should be considered a crime, there are measures that can be taken to "resuscitate" your cigar, as long as the cigar's wrapper isn't damaged and the tobacco hasn't flaked to dust. In fact, when cured tobacco is shipped from the farm to the rolling factory, it arrives dry and must be steamed before it can be worked. But don't do that with your cigar. Holding a dry cigar over a steam kettle will just make it soggy, and then it'll come apart. The moisture needs to be worked into the cigar at a much more gradual pace, or it'll be ruined.

If your dry cigar is wrapped in cellophane, leave it wrapped. Taking it out may damage the leaf wrapper and render it unsmokable. To bring back its freshness, put it in a plastic container with the top off, and place it as high in your bathroom as you can while you shower. Before the steam in the room dissipates, put the plastic cover on, trapping the steam inside. This should be done in addition to regular humidification procedures like keeping a glass fileld with a sponge and distilled water in the container. Do this day after day until you can feel and smell the freshness return to the cigar. You'll know it's ready when you poke it and the wrapper leaf gives a little to the touch, but rebounds to its original shape. With the current price of a premium cigar—and all the love and care and handicraft that's been put into making it—I think it's worth trying to save the cigar's life.

A word about pests

They're found infrequently and they usually pose no concern to the cigar consumer, but I'd be remiss if I didn't mention the tobacco beetle. This tiny insect is much more of a bane to the wholesaler than it is to the smoker, and all importers and manufacturers I know go to great effort and expense to keep their warehouses and shops free of the pest, which can render thousands of dollars' worth of stock worthless over a period of time.

Smokers should keep in mind that the tobacco beetle is no threat to human health. It's found in many cereal mills, and people can even eat it without danger—not that you'd want to! The beetle lays its eggs in tobacco and then eats its way out—never into the tobacco. If you find a tiny worm, it's best to discard it along with the affected cigar and wipe up any dust you might find—it could contain the beetle's tiny eggs.

Ironically, presence of the tobacco beetle in your cigar stock is something of a compliment. The insect has sophisticated taste in tobacco and only inhabits the finest leaf.

Preparing to smoke

Now that you've taken the time and attention to care properly for your cigar, it's time to get down to the essence of it all—smoking it. But first, the last few steps of preparation are crucial. Here are some tips to get you on your way.

■ Every fine cigar needs its crown cut before it is smoked. The crown is the part of the cigar that goes into your mouth. Maybe you've smoked a cigar that came with a precut hole, but most premium handmade cigars have a special cap made of a small, separate piece of tobacco placed over the end to strengthen it and keep the cigar securely rolled, and the puncture through which you draw the smoke is left for you to make.

Every fine cigar needs its crown cut
before it is smoked.

I prefer a V, or notch, cutter to slice the crown of my cigar. It allows deep penetration—about a quarter of an inch—yet maintains the integrity of the crown.

There are a number of cutting tools available on the market, providing many interesting and nearly equally effective choices for the cigar smoker. They come at a variety of prices and can be very fashionable and highbrow, like a 24-carat gold cutter or an art deco sterling-silver hole puncher. Or they can be plastic promotional items, given away free of charge or sold for a nominal fee by a tobacconist, to advertise a line of cigars or a certain shop.

Of all the choices available, I prefer a V, or notch, cutter to cut the crown of my cigar. Notch cutters are the approximate size of large nail clippers and can be carried in your pocket and used anywhere. To use a notch cutter, place the crown of the cigar in the hole at the end of the tool and depress the blade, which will slice a V–shaped notch in the cigar end. I like the notch cutter because it allows deep penetration—about a quarter of an inch—into the crown of the cigar, clearing out a large area from which the smoke can be drawn, yet it maintains the integrity of the crown. If you cut that deeply with any other type of cutter, the smoke would billow everywhere, bits of tobacco would flake off in your mouth, and there's a good chance the cigar would begin to unravel due to damage to the finely crafted head. In any event, you never want to cut below the crown because you'll simply ruin the cigar; you want to lop off just enough to reveal the filler leaves.

The guillotine-style cutter is probably the most common. It's basically a flat, sliding blade that shears off the top of the cigar's crown. I think it has all the problems I've just listed, but if you're cautious you can make it work. Be extra careful to line up only the very, very tip of the crown—about an eighth of inch—in the guillotine before pushing the blade through it—too much and you're in for trouble. You'll be spitting out bits of

Off with their heads! (Cigar heads, that is.)

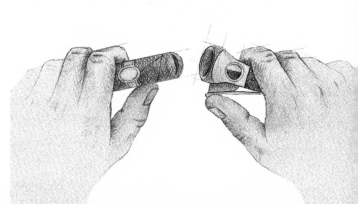

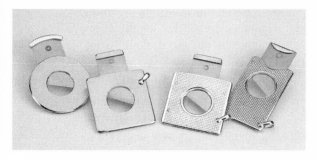

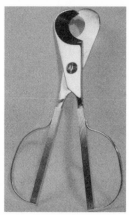

(Above, left) **Hand-held guillotine cutters are the most common type.**

(Left) **Marie Antoinette would shiver to see this tabletop guillotine cutter. Just stick your cigar in the hole and let the blade fall.**

(Above) **Scissors have two blades that surround the head of the cigar and cut simultaneously toward the middle.**

tobacco and wishing your cigar end would stay rolled. Guillotine cutters are made to be portable—many promotional cutters are guillotine-style—but some of the most fun and imaginative cigar accessories I've seen are heavier, tabletop guillotine cutters. Some are miniature versions of the real guillotines made famous during the French Revolution. Cigar heads will roll!

Another impressive-looking implement among the available cutting tools is the cigar scissors. They're just like small scissors you might use to clip your fingernails, only with rounded blades. They take a steady hand to operate, but as long as you're careful to cut just the right amount off the crown, you'll do fine. The scissor style has all the advantages of the single-blade guillotine, but has the added feature of possessing two blades that surround the head of the cigar and cut simultaneously toward the middle, as opposed to slicing across from one side like the guillotine does.

Hole punchers can be neat and effective, too—not the kind you find in a stationery store, but the kind that are specially made for cigars and remove a small, round portion of the head of the cigar—but don't use a toothpick or fingernail to gouge a hole in the cigar. Those methods just bunch the tobacco around the hole and make it more difficult to draw smoke through it. Knives have the potential to be sloppy, but could work in a pinch. And unless you've been doing it for years or can't get hold of a real cutter, don't try biting the end off the cigar. This very often results in errant pieces of tobacco flaking off and a questionable draw on the end of your cigar. If you want to emulate the tough guys of the old movies, there's no better way. Just make sure you don't ruin a perfectly good cigar in the process.

■ Keep the ring on or take it off? Cigar makers will unanimously urge you to keep it on. And why not? It's free advertising! Usually, though, it's best to leave it on, because you might damage the delicate wrapper leaf with your fingernail or the band itself might be slightly stuck to the cigar, ripping the wrapper when it's forced off. If this happens, the integrity of the cigar's draw will be broken and the cigar will be hard to puff on.

The English consider it impolite to leave the ring on the cigar while you smoke. Perhaps they think it's rude to advertise, or

(Top and bottom left) **Hole punchers slice out a nice round hole in the head of the cigar.**

(Below) **Here are examples of what cigar heads look like after being properly cut using different methods. On the left, two cigars cut with a guillotine; in the middle, two Vs sliced with a notch cutter; and on the right, results of the hole puncher.**

they believe it's bragging if you're smoking a fine cigar
and leave the brand name attached for all to see. If in
doubt, and you're in Britain, do what the British do.

If you do find yourself in England, or you're otherwise
lighting up a cigar you'd rather not advertise, keep in
mind that it's much easier to get the band off the cigar
after you've been puffing for a while. The heat will
loosen the glue on the back of the band and make sliding it off the cigar that much less risky.

Time to light up!

Every cigar is a different
sensual experience.
Here's how to elicit the
most enjoyment out of every smoke.

- Never light a cigar with a fluid lighter or a candle. The taste of the fluid
or the wax will taint the taste of the cigar. Use a butane lighter or a wood-
en match, or, if you're using a sulfur-tipped match, wait for the sulfur to
burn off before holding your cigar near it. Disposable lighters do the trick
just as well as the more expensive ones. Before lighting the end, or "tuck"
as it's called, run the flame up and down the length of the cigar a few
times. This gets the tobacco oils flowing. Never touch the tuck to the flame
itself, but hold the cigar over the flame and rotate it, letting it heat slowly
and evenly. The cigar end will flare when the cigar is ready to be
smoked, not necessarily when you want it to. So be patient. Make
sure the entire end of the cigar is lit evenly before you quit the lighting procedure. That will ensure an
even burn for the length of your smoke.

- Don't rush it! Enjoy your cigar. A
large cigar may take an hour or more
to smoke. Even the average cigar lasts
about half an hour. Take the time to
savor the flavor. Smoke slowly. If you
puff too fiercely, the cigar will become
hot and unpleasant. Don't flick the ash
off every time it grows. The ash actually protects and nurtures the flame and
makes for a more even burn and a
smoother smoke.

It's also fun to smoke a cigar on the golf course or while fishing, but keep in mind that wind and other outdoor conditions fan the cigar's flame, causing it to burn hotter and taste somewhat more bitter.

■ Some folks never put down their cigars, but for those who do, special ashtrays are available that are equipped with extra-wide rims to hold the longest, fattest cigars. This way the cigar flame is kept off the bottom of the ashtray, enabling the ash to remain on the end of the cigar.

■ You can smoke your cigar as far down as you prefer, but I usually stop after about two-thirds of the cigar is gone. Keep in mind that tobacco is its own best filter, and the oils that you draw toward you with each puff accumulate in the cigar and alter its flavor. When you smoke past the two-thirds mark, your cigar will taste a lot stronger. If you like that stronger flavor, go right ahead and keep smoking. But if you want to remember your cigar for the true nature of its savor, put it down at about the two-thirds mark.

■ If your cigar goes out, you have about twenty or thirty minutes to relight it. After that, the oils in the tobacco will have crystallized and the cigar will taste stale and sour and emit a foul odor.

■ When you're done, don't stub out the cigar, but let it die with dignity in the ashtray. Stubbing it releases an unpleasant aroma. For similar reasons, don't let it sit in the ashtray for longer than twenty or thirty minutes or the sour smell will begin to fill the room. Be kind to those around you and dispose of what's left of the cigar.

I think you'll be surprised how much more you'll enjoy cigar smoking once you know some of the little tricks of the trade. As is true with many of the finer things in life, you'll find that practice makes perfect—and the practicing is so much fun!

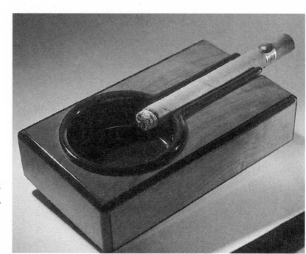

A fine cigar deserves a fine ashtray.

Chapter Five
Planning and Enjoying a Cigar Dinner

C igar dinners are a celebration of
camaraderie, a long, leisurely evening
replete with the best life has to offer—
fine wine, fine food,

fine spirits, fine fellowship, and fine cigars. At its best, a cigar dinner is not just any random menu thrown together and accompanied by whatever cigars happen to be lying around. Rather, it's a carefully planned, meticulously structured event that weds cigar to wine to food in a complementary mélange that excites the palate, encourages experimentation, and promotes the vigorous exchange of ideas.

As far as I can tell, the tradition of the after-dinner cigar goes back as far as the use of tobacco itself. It's not difficult to imagine those first Mayan smokers of antiquity enjoying a good handmade cigar after a hearty stew of corn meal and beans in a Guatemalan village. Maybe they even had their own smoking den and wore special clothing, like the Europeans of the eighteenth and nineteenth centuries, who donned after-dinner smoking jackets and smoking caps to keep the smell of their less-than-smooth cigars off their waistcoats and wigs. But even with such a colorful history behind it, the contemporary cigar dinner didn't take off until a hotelier with a nose for innovation was struck with a fortuitous brainstorm.

The modern cigar dinner

One day in 1983, Henry Schielein, manager of the Ritz-Carlton Hotel in Boston, was enjoying a cigar in the hotel lobby when a guest jokingly mentioned how nice it would be if he were allowed to relish a good smoke in the hotel's famous restaurant. A lightbulb went on over Henry's head. There was a little-used tea room off in a corner of the hotel that was closed after six o'clock in the evening, and Henry decided to open it as a lounge for cigar smokers. The idea was a huge success, and when he moved to California to manage the Ritz-Carlton in Newport Beach, Henry decided to combine the smoking lounge and the restaurant for a special event he called a cigar dinner. Posh doesn't come anywhere near describing the black-tie dinner Henry put on. Many Hollywood stars showed up, puffing away at their favorite cigars; invitations were as scarce as spare Super Bowl tickets.

Owing to all the movie stars present and the attendant pomp, the Newport Beach Ritz-Carlton cigar dinner got a lot of press, and imitators began to spring up all over the country. But Henry remained king of the cigar dinner. He outdid himself after he moved to Maui and took over the Grand Waialea Hotel. The cable TV Food Channel sent Robin Leech out there for a special program, and I was privileged enough to be interviewed by him along with the hotel's chef. The dinner started off with cocktails and cigars on the lawn overlooking the blue Pacific; then we were seated at U-shaped tables, which provided for terrific opportunities to get to know the other diners. We were served by white-gloved waiters, one for each guest, who were impeccable in their precision. The headwaiter would nod and thirty plates would hit the table at the same time. After dinner, we retired to the pool room for billiards, cigars, and camaraderie. It was Henry's style to provide different cigars during the cocktail hour and with dessert. He let the guests choose which ones they wanted to smoke.

Cigar dinners have evolved somewhat since then. Now, when Nat Sherman co-sponsors such an event, we prescribe specific cigars for each course of the meal and work closely with the chef and sommelier to produce the perfect ambiance.

Guidelines for a successful cigar dinner

Since the courtship of wine, food, and cigars is so important to the success of the cigar dinner, all preparations for each of these aspects should be made in tandem. Keep in mind that cigar dinners are not affairs meant for white wine and subtle foods. Though there's no reason why a memorable cigar dinner can't feature a vegetarian menu, an effort should be made to serve foods with some kick.

Traditionally, meat and game have been the centerpiece for the most satisfying cigar dinners, with peppery wine-reduction sauces and salads with spicy dressings, such as Roquefort or bleu cheese.

Before I give you more details, there are a few general things to keep in mind when planning which cigars to offer with each course. Generally speaking, you want to start with a milder

For Women Only

The popularity of cigar dinners and the increasing number of women who indulge in cigar smoking has spawned a new phenomenon: the women-only cigar dinner. The twenty-six Morton's of Chicago steak houses across the country held such an event simultaneously on February 18, 1996, and the Manhattan cigar dinner drew sixty women at $95 a head. In addition to the four-course dinner, wine, and four cigars, guests received a coupon to a local dry cleaner.

cigar and progress to more full-bodied selections as the evening proceeds, and you want to take into account the length of time you've set aside for smoking. It makes sense, for instance, to serve a longer, wider cigar during pre-dinner cocktails, when you have an hour or more in which to smoke, and a shorter cigar after the salad is eaten, when a twenty-minute break between courses is a more reasonable expectation.

Here are some more general guidelines, along with two suggested menus for your own cigar dinner. These are simply guidelines, and I urge you to find your own favorite foods to marry to your favorite cigars. Since cigar dinners can be elegant, black-tie affairs, or they can be unhurried, casual gatherings of good friends, I've provided two sample menus. Dinner A is the fancier one; it's based on a cigar dinner Nat Sherman did at the Culinary Institute of America in January 1996. I've included recipes from the Culinary Institute, so if you want to duplicate that cigar dinner, you can. Under each course heading you'll find the food, then the beverage, then the cigar.

The cocktail hour

For apéritifs, choose either a single-malt scotch or Champagne. We use single-malt scotch and cognac as accompaniments to cigar tastings at our Manhattan store, and the compliments always flow. For this starter phase of the evening, serve a cigar with a Connecticut shade-grown wrapper, which will have enough body to stand up to the heartiness of the scotch or the bubbles of the Champagne, but won't numb the taste buds for later courses. A mellow Lonsdale–about 6½ inches, with a 43 ring gauge–should be large enough to last through the cocktail hour.

Cigar enthusiasts gather for scotch, cognac, and cigars on the Club Floor of the Nat Sherman store on Fifth Avenue in Manhattan.

My Dream Dinner

Here's what I'd serve at a cigar dinner if the chef and sommelier let me take over and dictate the whole affair. Keep in mind that I'm a man of fairly simple tastes, and I'm no wine expert, so I can't tell you what specific vintages I especially like, but here goes:

COCKTAIL HOUR

Champagne

Pastry-wrapped fish canapés

Nat Sherman Hampton (7 x 50 with a colorado-claro Connecticut wrapper)

APPETIZER

Chardonnay

Pea soup

Salad with a thick, garlicky vinaigrette dressing

Nat Sherman Chelsea (6½ x 38 with a colorado wrapper from Mexico)

DINNER

Merlot

Venison in a wine-and-mushroom sauce

Creamed spinach

Glazed baby carrots

DESSERT

Port and coffee

Chocolate mousse or cheesecake

Nat Sherman Dakota (7½ x 49 with a colorado-maduro Cameroon wrapper)

These ingredients make a memorable
cigar dinner: Fine wine, fine food, fine spirits,
fine fellowship, and fine cigars.

■ **Dinner A:**

Pâté de foie gras with assortment of breads

Sherry, Champagne, and single-malt scotch

Nat Sherman Harrington (5 x 47 with a colorado-maduro wrapper from Ecuador)

■ **Dinner B:**

Antipasto: Italian meats, cheeses, and marinated vegetables with focaccia bread

Champagne and single-malt scotch

Macanudo Vintage II (6½ x 43 with a Connecticut wrapper)

Soup or salad

I like peppery salad dressings, or dressings with sharp cheeses, and I think they stand up much better during a night where you're bombarding your taste buds with sensations. Try a Pouilly Fuissé or Pinot Noir with salad, and after salad it's time for a Robusto or a Corona. These sizes–5 x 50 or 5½ x 42– will provide a relatively short smoke. This cigar should be a little more full-bodied than the mellower Connecticut wrapper, but still won't be so powerful its taste dwarfs what comes next. An interesting choice may be a cigar with a good Mexican wrapper, which so often is smooth enough not to take over but offers just enough suggestion of spice to make for an enjoyable intermezzo experience.

■ **Dinner A:**

Wood-fired vine-leaf-wrapped smoked salmon with red wine vinaigrette

Onion soup gratiné

Sauvignon Blanc

Nat Sherman Murray Hill No. 7 (6 x 38, with a Connecticut wrapper)

■ **Dinner B:**

Mesclun salad with Roquefort cheese and balsamic vinaigrette

Pinot Noir

Santa Damiana No. 500 (5 x 50 with a Connecticut wrapper)

Main course

With the main course, you want a wine that's a notch up in both flavor and body, like a Bordeaux, a Zinfandel, or a Cabernet. The food should be as full-bodied as the wine–it has to be distinctive enough to make an impression. Follow the food with a larger cigar, something with a slightly darker wrapper, like a Cameroon. Colorado wrappers provide an excellent complement to a robust meal. Serve a slightly larger cigar here, perhaps a 6 x 47.

■ **Dinner A:**

Tenderloin of beef with Bernaise sauce, garlic mashed potatoes, and French green beans

OR

Marinated grilled duck breast, roasted red potatoes, and French green beans

Merlot

Nat Sherman University (6 x 50 with a colorado-claro wrapper)

■ **Dinner B:**

Ravioli filled with lobster and radicchio in tomato sauce

OR

Osso Buco with mashed potatoes and French green beans

Chianti

Partagas Limited Reserve Regale (6½ x 48 with a colorado-maduro Cameroon wrapper)

Dessert

The last cigar of the evening, served with dessert and coffee, should be the most full-bodied of them all. A large-ring-gauge Cameroon, or a hearty maduro, makes a terrific finale. You'll want a cigar with a flavor strong enough to savor after you've given your mouth something of a workout over the course of the evening, so try a cigar in the 7 x 50 range. Cognac or Armagnac work well, too. Avoid exotic-flavored cordials, as they compete rather than complement the taste of the after-dinner cigar.

■ **Dinner A:**

Chocolate mousse

Madeira and coffees

Nat Sherman Tribune (7½ x 50 with a maduro Connecticut wrapper)

■ **Dinner B:**

Death by Chocolate cake with strawberries

Port, brandy, and coffees

Excalibur No. 1 by Hoyo de Monterrey (7¼ x 54 with a maduro Connecticut wrapper)

Cigar dinners should be fun, and part of the attraction for me is the discussion around the table as the evening goes on. I love to compare one cigar to another with my fellow diners, and relate how we each respond to

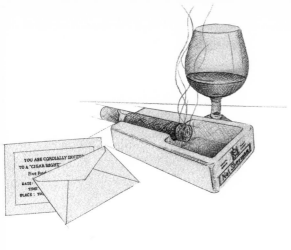

A cigar dinner can be a formal black-tie occasion, or it can be an informal gathering of friends at home around a roaring fireplace.

the selections offered. I love to talk about how the cigars complement or contrast with the spirits and wine being served. I love to chat about how each adds–or perhaps detracts–from the food, and how the cigars compare with others we've all smoked. A little friendly disagreement is not to be avoided–it's to be encouraged! As long as the debate doesn't get too technical or clinical or overly serious, I have a good time. So should you.

Your own cigar dinner

Not long ago I received a letter from a group of ten guys in Upper Michigan who meet once a month for their own cigar dinner. They get together in a cabin in the woods, eat a fine meal, and sit around a roaring fire in their flannel shirts and blue jeans and smoke cigars. They said they knew they were an obscure and very small group, but they lived 400 miles from the nearest tobacconist. Was there anything I could do to help them? Sure, I said. Could I join them?

I think the ideal cigar dinner would be like that–a meal shared with friends at home or in a low-key atmosphere, with two specially chosen cigars. That's all you really need. The four or five cigars served at the swankier affairs is fun, but could be a bit too many. Nobody loves cigars more than I do, but I rarely smoke four or five in a single night! You'd have a thin, light apéritif cigar, with a Connecticut shade-grown wrapper, to accompany cocktails; Champagne or wine before sitting down to dinner; and then a dessert cigar, long and big and robust, with a darker wrapper, to complement a cup of coffee and something sweet at the end of the meal.

Along with good friends and good conversation, that's my idea of heaven.

Recipes for Your Own Cigar Dinner

The three recipes that follow are from the renowned Culinary Institute of America, which held a cigar dinner featuring Nat Sherman cigars. Try them at home.

ONION SOUP GRATINÉ

3 lbs. onions, sliced thin
¼ cup oil
½ cup Calvados
1 gallon low-fat chicken broth
1¼ lbs. Gruyere cheese, grated
salt
pepper
croutons

1 Sauté the onions in oil until browned. Add a little oil if necessary to prevent burning.

2 Deglaze the pan with the Calvados. Add the broth.

3 Simmer until onions are tender.

4 Season with salt and pepper.

5 Garnish each portion with croutons. Top generously with grated cheese and brown under broiler, or bake in a moderate oven until lightly browned.

Yields one gallon.

Allow me to (again) recommend the Nat Sherman Murray Hill No. 7 with a Connecticut wrapper to complement this recipe.

MARINATED GRILLED DUCK BREAST

10 duck breasts, boned and halved

MARINADE:
1 cup soy sauce
1 cup water
1 tbsp. dark sesame oil
1 tbsp. hoisin sauce
1 tbsp. ginger, coarsely chopped
1 tbsp. garlic, minced
salt
pepper

1 Trim the duck breasts if necessary; place in a pan.

2 Combine all ingredients for marinade, and pour mixture over the duck, reserving some marinade to baste duck while grilling. Turn the breasts in marinade to cover evenly. Let duck breasts marinate in the refrigerator for several hours or overnight.

3 Grill duck breasts. Brush with marinade while cooking.

4 Slice duck breasts on the diagonal and finish on the grill.

Yields 10 servings.

Recommended cigar: Nat Sherman University with a colorado claro wrapper.

CHOCOLATE MOUSSE

10 oz. chocolate, semisweet
3 tbsp. butter
5 egg yolks, pasteurized
¼ cup sugar
5 egg whites, pasteurized
2 tbsp. dark rum or vanilla, to taste
1 cup heavy cream, whipped

1 Combine chocolate and butter; melt over a warm burner.

2 Whip egg yolks and half the sugar to full volume.

3 Whip egg whites and the remaining sugar to full volume.

4 Fold egg whites into egg yolks.

5 Fold butter-chocolate mixture into egg-sugar mixture.

6 Add rum or vanilla and fold in whipped cream.

7 Scoop into desired serving dishes.

Yields 10 servings.

Recommended cigar: Nat Sherman Tribune with a maduro Connecticut wrapper.

Chapter Six

Seek and You Shall Find: A Guide to Cigar Retailers

What good is the best cigar on earth if you can't find it? Don't laugh—once you've settled on the cigar you want to smoke, it often can be very difficult to locate it. That's why

I've assembled this list of cigar retailers, which includes just about every state in the union.

When you mention a specific city or town in the United States, most people get a mental picture even if they haven't visited there. Maybe they see a certain famous street, a well-known landmark, or a sports facility. But to me, this country is one big tobacco shop. Mention "Chicago" and most people picture skyscrapers along Lake Michigan, the Sears Tower, or maybe Wrigley Field. I see Diana Gits, one of the world's most effective cigar promoters, outside her Up Down smoke shop, revving her Harley-Davidson, en route to another of her famous cigar dinners. Say "Detroit" and folks will picture the smokestacks and factories of the Big Three automakers, or the skyscrapers of the Renaissance Center reflecting the sunlight. I see Max Burns, the old union-organizer-turned-tobacconist, who once told me in his Humidor One smoke shop that with the recent boom in the popularity of the cigar it took him forty years to be an overnight success. That's just me. That's how crazy I am about cigars and about the cigar business.

Creative merchandisers have contributed immeasurably to the popularity of cigars, and with the increased popularity has come a new and continually improving product. Cigars haven't always been as trendy as they are today, and many of these sellers had to weather some pretty tough times. Some of them, like Max Burns, branched out into other lines, like leather goods or, like J.R. Tobacco, perfume. But they survived, as Max says, to become "overnight successes." Some of those folks deserve mention here.

Lew Rothman of J.R. Tobacco honed a supermarket approach to the marketing of cigars, with discount pricing and a wide range of products. He's as responsible as anyone for the current popularity of cigars.

For years, Thompson Cigar of Miami almost singlehandedly kept the Ybor City and Tampa cigar manufacturers in the black with its mail-order business.

Frank Llaneza not only has been a phenomenal cigar designer, but when Ybor City died out in the early 1980s, he started a trend and unearthed a gold mine of terrific tobacco when he moved production facilities to Honduras.

Not enough homage has been paid to Ed and Carl Kolpin, who started the Tinder Box chain, the first tobacco-store franchises, in 1970. Their first store is still open, on Wilshire Boulevard in Santa Monica, California. The Kolpins developed everything, from the store design to the negotiation of leases for individual franchises. They created places to sell good cigars, many of which still exist. If you were a humidor manufacturer or a pipe maker or cigar-cutter maker, you could clear a healthy profit with a single contract from the Tinder Box people. The late Ed Kolpin was loved by many and hated by just as many, but he meant a lot to the tobacco industry, and he never got his due.

The love of cigars is the common denominator here; everyone is enthralled with the romance and passion of it. If these folks hadn't developed a winning merchandising strategy and stayed in business through the lean years, the success of the cigar industry we enjoy today and the satisfaction it brings to millions of people would never have taken place.

INTERNATIONAL

BRAZIL

Lenat Com. Imp. Ltd.
Av. Brig. Faria Lima
1191. LJ X44-CX315
São Paulo, Brazil 01451.000
011-815-5835

CANADA

Brigham Enterprises
25 Ripley Avenue
Toronto
Ontario, Canada
M6S 3P2
416-762-7278

Empire Tobacco Company
P.O. Box 22100
343 Wellington Road
London
Ontario, Canada
N6C 5V3
519-679-2523

Havana House
Cigars & Tobacco
9 Davies Avenue
Toronto
Ontario, Canada
M4M 2A6
416-406-6644

Havana Tobacconist
2901 Bayview Avenue
Bayview Village Shopping
  Center
Willowdale
Ontario, Canada
M2K1E6
416-733-9736

**La Tienda/Rialta Trading
  Inc.**
8426 109 Street
Edmonton
Alberta, Canada
T6G 1E2
403-439-5108

Thomas Hinds Tobacconist
8 Cumberland Street
Toronto
Province, Ontario
M4W 1J5
416-757-0237

Tobacco Haven
595 Bay Street
P. O. Box 50
Ontario, Canada
M5G 2C2
416-593-6655

Wiff 'N Puff
486 Village Green Avenue
London
Ontario,Canada
N6J123
519-472-1244

Winston & Holmes Limited
138 Cumberland Street
Toronto
Ontario, Canada
M5R 1A6
416- 968-1290

CHILE

Tabaqueira M & N
Neuwirth y Henriquez
  Limtada
Manquehue Sur No. 31 Local
Santiago, Chile

ENGLAND

Alfred Dunhill Limited
30 Duke Street
St. James, SW1 London
171-499-9566

Davidoff of London
35 St. James's Street
London, England SW1A
 1HDD
071-930-3079

**Fox/Lewis Cigar
 Merchants**
19, St. James Street
SW1 London
171-930-3787

FRANCE

La Corche Selva
5, Rue Roger Dion
Bcoise, France 41000
33-54-780259

A Casa del Hobano
69, Boulevard Saint-
 Germain
Paris, France
4549-2430

HOLLAND

The Old Man
Damstraat 7-16
Amsterdam, Holland
 10122M
113120270043

HONG KONG

Cohiba Cigar Divan
The Lobby
The Mandarin Oriental
 Hotel
Central Hong Kong
852-522-0111

ITALY

Regali Novelli
Via San Marcello, 39
Rome, Italy 00187
396-6792852

MALAYSIA

Havana Club
P1 Prestige Fllor, Level 4
Lot 10 Shopping Centre
50 Jalan Sultan Ismail
50250 Kuala Lumpur
Malaysia
03-245-5996

MEXICO

**Casa Del Tabacco, S.A. de
 C.V.**
Tennyson #18
Colonia Polanco C.P. 11560
Mexico, D.F.
525-2821184

Cigarrera La Moderna
Ventronic, S.A. de C.V.
Av. Oscar Wilde #244 Col.
Ind'l San Jemo
Monterrey, NL 64630
Mexico
8-347-1406

Cubanos en Cabo
Calle Manuel Doblado y
 Morelos
San Jose del Cabo
BCS, Mexico

**Tabacos Labraods, S.A. de
 C.V.**
184 Zacatecas - Colonia
 Roma
Mexico City, Mexico 06700

SAINT BARTHÉLEMY

Le Comptoir de Cigare
6, Rue de General de Gaulle
Gustavia
97113
Saint-Barthélemy FWI
590-275062

SWITZERLAND

Tabac Rhein
1, Rue de Mont-Blanc
CH-1201
Geneva, Switzerland
41-227329764

Gerard Pere et Fils
Hoetl Noga Hilton
19, Quai du Mont Blanc
Switzerland
41-227-32 65 11

DOMESTIC

ALABAMA

The Briary
Brookwood Village
No. 741-B
Birmingham, AL 35114
205-871-2839

Tobacco Barn
Route 13, Box 7
2101 Airport Road North
Jasper, AL 35501
205-221-4564

Tobacco Express
802 Highway 431 North
Boaz, AL 35957
205-593-2288

Tobacco Express
3290 Florence Boulevard
Box 62-B
Florence, AL 35630
205-764-7641

**Wetmore & Associates-
Tinder Box 215**
3484 Bel Air Mall
Mobile, AL 36606
205-473-1221

ALASKA

**Tobacco Cache of Alaska,
Inc.**
601 East Northern Lights
Boulevard
Suite L
Anchorage, AK 99503
907-279-9411

ARKANSAS

Davis's Smoke Shop
P.O. Box 1248
Russellville, AR 72801
501-968-6760

Discount Tobacco
P.O. Box 71
El Dorado, AR 71730
501-863-8191

Liquor Mart
7615 Rogers Avenue
Fort Smith, AR 72903
501-484-9463

The Pipe & Tobacco Shop
2908 South University
Broadmoor Shopping Center
Little Rock, AR 72204
501-562-7473

The Southern Gentleman
21 West Mountain
Fayetteville, AR 72701
501-521-1422

**Taylor's Pipe & Tobacco
Shop**
5340 Rogers Avenue
Fort Smith, AR 72903
501-452-1449

The Tobacco Shop
121 West Township Road,
#21
Fayetteville, AR 72703
501-444-8311

Tobacco Superstores
P.O. Box 1859
Forrest City, AR 72335
501-633-2044

ARIZONA

Action Products
3310 West Bell Road
Suite 150
Phoenix, AZ 85023
602-944-5133

Annie's
4500 North Oracle Road
Tucson, AZ 85705
520-749-5542

Churchill's Fine Cigars
5021 North 44th Street
Phoenix, AZ 85023
602-840-9080

D J's Smoke Shop
1815 West 1st Avenue
#115
Mesa, AZ 85202
602-464-8598

Ford & Haig Tobacconist
7076 East 5th Avenue
Scottsdale, AZ 85251
602-946-0608

MRN Limited
Head East
P.O. Box 17009
Tucson, AZ 85731
520-322-9929

The Sentinel Tobacconist
224 South Main Street
Suite 109
Yuma, AZ 85364
520-539-0003

Smoker's Haven, Inc.
5870 East Broadway #101
Tucson, AZ 85711
520-747-8989

Stag Tobacconist
9627A Metro Parkway West
Phoenix, AZ 85051
602-943-7517

Trails Department Store
5111 North 32nd Avenue
Phoenix, AZ 85017
602-336-8537

Ye Olde Pipe & Tobacco
2115 East Camelback Road
Phoenix, AZ 85016
602-955-7740

CALIFORNIA

A Man's World
40 Kentucky Street
Petaluma, CA 94952
707-778-9100

Bad Habits
3850 Fifth Avenue
San Diego, CA 92103
619-298-6340

Baker Street Tobacconist
3053 Jefferson Street
Napa, CA 94558
707-252-2766

Beverages & More
1100A Pleasant Valley Drive
Pleasant Hill, CA 94523
510-472-3506

**Beverly Hills Pipe &
Tobacco Co.**
218 North Beverly Drive
Beverly Hills, CA 90210
310-276-7358

The Big Easy
12604 Ventura Boulevard
Studio City, CA 91604
818-762-3279

Briar Patch Smokeshop
1689 Arden Way
Suite 2006
Sacramento, CA 95818
916-443-8466

Briar Rose
Carson Mall No. 537
20700 South Avalon
Boulevard
Carson, CA 90746
310-538-1018

California Tobacco Co., Ltd.
P.O. Box 14323
San Francisco, CA 94114
415-495-5900

Captain Hunt
851D
West Harbor Drive
San Diego, CA 92101
619-232 -2938

Century City Tobacco Shoppe
10250 Santa Monica Boulevard
Los Angeles, CA 90067
310-277-0760

Chic
Box 5365
Carmel, CA 93921
408-625-2442

The Cigar Company
380 South Lake Avenue
Pasadena, CA 91101
818-792-2112

Cigar Den
Fenton Marketing, Inc.
17933 Ventura Boulevard
Encino, CA 91316
818-706-2526

The Cigar Store
1005 Santa Barbara
Santa Barbara, CA 93101
805-640-1210

Cigar Warehouse
15141 Ventura Boulevard
Sherman Oaks, CA 91423
818-789-1401

Cigarette City/Havanas
1576 North 1st
Fresno, CA 93703
209-485-2825

Cigars Ltd.
5132 North Palm
Box 7624
Fresno, CA 93747
209-229-1555

The Customer Company
P.O. Box 886
Benicia, CA 94510
707-745-6691

Duffy's Liquor Store
329 Vernon Street
Roseville, CA 95678
916-783-3258

Ed's Pipe Shop
2729 Wilshire Boulevard
Santa Monica, CA 90403
213-828-4512

Edwards Tobaccos Ltd.
19301-B Saticoy Street
Reseda, CA 91335
818-349-2300

Gerry's Fine Cigars
2324 Brundage Lane
Bakersfield, CA 93304
805-633-1440

Glenoak Corp.
400 East Glenoaks Boulevard
Glendale, CA 91207
818-247-5544

Gourmet Faire
6102 Sunset Boulevard
Los Angeles, CA 90028
213-462-5371

Green Jug Fine Wines
6307 Platt Avenue
Woodland Hills, CA 91367
818-887-9463

Gus Smoke Shop
13420 Ventura Boulevard
Sherman Oaks, CA 91423
818-789-1401

Haight Street Tobacco
1827 Haight Street
San Francisco, CA 94117
415-221-3415

Hardwick's Briar Shoppe
Manchester Center
3402 North Blackstone, #124
Fresno, CA 93726
209-228-1389

The High Road
1463 Garnet Avenue
San Diego, CA 92109
619-273-7501

Hiland's Gifts & Tobacco
14340 Bolsa Chica
#F
Westminster, CA 92683
714-897-9216

Inner World
211 North Hill Street
Oceanside, CA 92054
619-722-3711

John T's Gifts for Him
1419-B Solano Mall
Fairfield, CA 94533
707-426-5566

Joint Private Venture
975 Fairway Drive
Walnut, CA 91789
909-595-8799

La Plata Cigars
1026 South Grand Avenue
Los Angeles, CA 90015
213-747-8561

Liberson's Gourmet International Tobaccos
10143 Riverside Drive
Toluca Lake, CA 91602
818-985-4310

Liberty Tobacco
7341 Clairmont Mesa Boulevard
Suite 110
San Diego, CA 92111
619-292-1772

Lil Havana
1011 Mason Street
#1
Vacaville, CA 95688
707-447-8678

Maxwell's Tobacco Shop
2500 East Imperial Highway
Suite 199
Brea, CA 92621
714-256-2344

Mission Pipe Shop
812 Town & Country Village Drive
San Jose, CA 95128
408-241-8868

Naples Pipe Shop
5662 East Second Street
Long Beach, CA 90803
310-439-8515

Palm Desert Tobacco & Gifts
Palm Desert Town Center
#G235
Palm Desert, CA 92260
619-340-3364

Phillip Dane's Cigar Lounge
9669 Little Santa Monica Boulevard
Beverly Hills, CA 90210
310-285-9945

The Piedmont Tobacconist
17 Glen Avenue
Oakland, CA 94611
510-652-PIPE

Politically Incorrect Tobacco & Gifts
1015 Gayley Avenue
#337
Los Angeles, CA 90024
310-448-9979

Romeo et Juliette
1198 Pacific Coast Highway
Seal Beach, CA 90740
310-430-2331

San-Vay Corp. dba Hi-Time Liquor
250 Ogle Street
Costa Mesa, CA 92627
714-650-8463

Sherlock's Haven
1 Embarcadero Center
San Francisco, CA 94111
415-362-1405

Smoker's Depot
145 Jamacha Road
El Cajon, CA 92021
619-440-3400

Telford's Pipe Shop
119 Strawberry Village
Mill Valley, CA 94947
415-388-0440

Tinder Box (#107)
Crystal Court South Coast Plaza
3333 Bear Street
Costa Mesa, CA 92626
714-540-8262

The Tinder Box (#122)
Tyler Mall, No. 3624
Tyler Street and Magnolia Avenue
Riverside, CA 92503
909-689-4401

The Tinder Box (#147)
Sunrise Mall, No. 6144
Greenback Lane and Sunrise Boulevard
Citrus Heights, CA 95610
916-725-3231

Tinder Box (#152)
Parkway Plaza
329 Parkway Plaza
El Cajon, CA 92020
619-440-3400

Tinder Box (#335)
North County Fair #157
200 Via Rancho Parkway
Escondido, CA 92025
619-745-9230

The Tinder Box–Wilshire
The Squire
346 Coddingtown Center
Santa Rosa, CA 95401
707 -573-8544

Tobacco Loft
1920 Contra Costa Boulevard
Pleasant Hill, CA 94523
510-686-3440

Tobacco Pipe
7802 Foothill Boulevard
Sunland, CA 91040
818-352-3210

Tobacco Trader
4722 1/4 Admiralty Way
Marina Del Rey, CA 90292
310-823-5831

Tower Pipes & Cigars
2518 Land Park Drive
Sacramento, CA 95818
916-443-8466

Ugly Al's Fine Cigars
7239 Corbin Avenue
Canoga Park, CA 91306
818-709-1525

Village Smoke Shoppe
31260 La Baya Drive
Unit C
Westlake Village, CA 91362
818-707-3207

The Baggage Claim, Inc.
307 South Galena Street
Aspen, CO 81611
303-442-5900

Cigar & Tobacco World
5227 Leetsdale Drive
Denver, CO 80222
303-321-7308

Cigarette Express
6630 West Colfax Avenue
Lakewood, CO 80214
303-235-2755

Durango Smoke Shop
113 West College Drive
Durango, CO 81301
970-226-5311

Eads News & Smoke Shop
1715 28th Street
Boulder, CO 80301
303-442-5900

Edward's Pipe & Tobacco
3307 South College Avenue
#102-B
Ft. Collins, CO 80525-4196
970-226-5311

Jerri's Tobacco Shop
1616 Glenarm Street
Denver, CO 80202
303-825-3522

Prince Philip's Pipes & Tobacco
Tamarac Square
7777 East Hampden
Denver, CO 80231
303-695-1959

Stag of Colorado, Ltd.
Stag Tobacconist
750 Citadel Drive East
Suite 2214
Colorado Springs, CO 80909
719-596-5363

The Tobacco Leaf
7111 West Alameda Avenue
Lakewood, CO 80226
303-274-8721

The Tobacconist
218 Maroon, #C
Box 1845
Crested Butte, CO 81224
970-247-9115

Aperitif of Canton
50 Albany Turnpike
Canton, CT 06019
203-693-9373

Cloud Nine
333 North Main Street
Moosup, CT 06354
203-564-5797

Connoiseur's Delight
83 Wooster Heights Road
Danbury, CT 06810
203-730-0107

De La Concha of Hartford
1 Civic Center Plaza
Hartford, CT 06103
203-527-4291

Have A Cigar! Tobacco Shop
980 Sullivan Avenue
South Windsor, CT 06074
203-644-5800

Owl Shop
268 College Street
New Haven, CT 06510
203-624-3250

The Smoke Shop
Village Green
Southbury, CT 06488
203-264-5075

Smokin' Sounds
1026 High Ridge Road
Stamford, CT 06905
203-329-8525

Margate Newstand
5430 West Atlantic
Boulevard
Margate, FL 33063
305-968-7563

Mintz Inc., The Brass Pipe
2573 South U.S. 1
Ft. Pierce, FL 34982
407-461-7451

Mr. D's Pipe & Tobacco
Shop
27001 U.S. 19 North,
Suite 1049
Clearwater, FL 34621
813-796-1220

Nightrain
8 South Atlantic
Daytona Beach, FL 32118
904-238-3640

NML Pipes Direct
12159 Cuddington Court
Wellington, FL 33414
407-743-0153

Ol' Times
124 West Pine Street
Orlando, FL 32801
407-425-7879

The Pipe Den
P.O. Box 602
1426 20th Street
Vero Beach, FL 32960
407-569-1154

Pipe & Pouch Smoke Shop
53 North Orange Avenue
Orlando, FL 32801
407-841-7980

Rainbow Connection
10482 SW 72nd Streeet
Miami, FL 33173
305-596-0614

R. Quirantes Cigar Co.
4122 West 12th Avenue
Hialeah, FL 33012
305-821-6181

San Pedro Premium Cigar
Co.
P.O. Box 15764
Tallahassee, FL 32317-5764
904-509-0114

Sir Richard Tobacco
Shoppe
2320 McGregor Boulevard
Ft. Myers, FL 33901
941-332-7722

The Smoke Shop
106 Crossroads Center
Sarasota, FL 34239
813-955-6433

Smoke Shop II
Omni International
1601 Biscayne Boulevard
Miami, FL 33132
305-358-1886

Smoke Shop Etc.
2810-2 Sharer Road
Tallahassee, FL 32312
904-385-9669

The Smoke Shop, Inc.
4625 Tamiami Trail North
Naples, FL 33940
813-435-1862

Smoke & Snuff
3899 Ulmerton Road
Clearwater, FL 34622
813-573-5601

Smoker's Gallery
The Galleria Mall
2356 East Sunrise Boulevard
Ft. Lauderdale, FL 33304
305-561-0002

Smoker's World, Inc.
20097 Biscayne Boulevard
North Miami Beach, FL
33180
305-931-1117

Sugar Daddy's Psychedelic
Shop
1676 South Congress Avenue
#48
Palm Springs, FL 33461
407-642-0396

Tabaceria
307 Merritt Square Mall
Merritt Island, FL 32952
407-452-4811

Tampa Rico Cigars
1901 13th Street
Tampa, FL 33605
813-247-6738

Tobacco Cove
3849 Bay Meadows Road
Jacksonville, FL 32217
904-731-2890

Tobacco Depot
23038 State Road 54
Lutz, FL 33549
813-948-3844

Ted's News Inc.
8744 Mills Drive
Miami, FL 33183
305-274-6397

Thompson Cigar Company
5401 Hangar Court
Tampa, FL 33634
813-884-6344

The Tinder Box (#182)
Orlando Fashion Square
3251 East Colonial Drive
Orlando, FL 32803
407-894-0022

The Tinder Box (#188)
2133 University Square Mall
Tampa, FL 33612
813-971-0623

The Tinder Box (#199)
2455 West International
Speedway Boulevard
Suite 401
Daytona Beach, FL 32114
904-253-0708

The Tinder Box (#239)
Cordova Mall
5100 North 9th Avenue
Pensacola, FL 32504
904-477-4131

Tobacco Emporium, Inc.
7451 Park Boulevard
Pinellas Park, FL 34665
813-544-0354

The Tobacco Hut
49036 South Madison Street
Elfers Square
New Port Richey, FL 34652
813-842-2139

The Tobacconist
119 Bullard Parkway
Temple Terrace, FL 33617
813-989-3133

T- Shirt Cellar, Inc.
14600 Front Beach Road
Panama City Beach, FL
32413
904-234-6361

Vistana Development
8001 Vistana Centre Drive
Suite 210
Orlando, FL 32821-6321
407-239-3700

The Wharf Pipe & Tobacco
Shop
973 Atlantic Boulevard
Atlantic Beach, FL 32233
904-246-8616

White Rabbit
4037 SW 96th Avenue
Miami, FL 33165
305-551-8722

Wholly Smokes & Unique
Gifts
11840 U.S. Highway 19
Port Richey, FL 34668-1053
813-863-0374

146

Wonderland
2126 Okeechobee Boulevard
West Palm Beach, FL 33409
402-689-1250

The Wooden Nickel of
Tampa, Inc.
1441 East Fletcher Avenue
Suite 141
Tampa, FL 33612
813-977-0904

Yab Yum, Inc.
25 Wall Street Place
Orlando, FL 32801
407-422-0019

Zelick's Tobacco Corp.
326 Lincoln Road
Miami Beach, FL 33139
305-538-1544

GEORGIA

Barnett's Newsstand
147 College Avenue
Athens, GA 30601
706-353-0530

Buckhead Fine Wine
3906 Roswell Road
Suite C
Atlanta, GA 30342
404-231-8566

Cigar Emporium
4719 Lower Roswell Road
Marietta, GA 30068
404-579-8280

The Cigar Merchant
9850 Nesbit Ferry Road
Suite 17
Alpharetta, GA 30202
404-689-1250

Cigar Villa
3599 Atlanta Road
Smyrna, GA 30080
413-433-1243

Clubhouse Cigars
6000 Medlock Bridge
Parkway
Suite B-100
Alpharetta, GA 30202
409-495-9330

Edward's Pipe & Tobacco
444 North Indian Creek
Drive
Clarkston, GA 30021
404-292-1721

The Junkman's Daughter
464 Moreland Avenue
Atlanta, GA 30307
404-577-3188

M & R Tobacco Shop
3711 Paul Street
Douglasville, GA 30135
404-920-2346

Merchant of Venice Ltd.
P.O. Box 93305
Atlanta, GA 30377-0305
404-659-5599

Royal Cigar Co.
1776 Peachtree Street NW
Atlanta, GA 30309
404-876-9422

This That and the Other
2040 Cobb Parkway
Atlanta, GA 30080
404-984-8801

The Tinder Box (#331)
Gwinnet Place Mall,
Suite 133
2100 Pleasant Hill Road
Duluth, GA 30136
404-813-1248

The Tinder Box At Lenox
3393 Peachtree Road NE
Atlanta, GA 30326
404-231-9853

Tobacco Express
3 Central Plaza
Suite 343
Rome, GA 30161
706-295-4204

The Ultimate Cigar
1381 Morrow Industrial
Boulevard
Morrow, GA 30260
404-968-9622

Vineville Beverage Shop
3117 Vineville Avenue
Macon, GA 31204
912-745-406

Ye Olde Tobacco Shoppe
131 West River Street
Savannah, GA 31401
912-236-9384

HAWAII

Tobacco & Gift Shop at the
Hyatt
2424 Kalakaua Avenue
Honolulu, HI 96815
808-923-8500

ILLINOIS

Al's Smoke Shop, Inc.
1 East Park Boulevard
Villa Park, IL 60181
708-279-2215

Arlington Pipe & Cigar
Shop
3 West Davis Street
Arlington Heights, IL 60005
708-255 -2263

Cigar Exchange
International
352 Lexington Drive
Buffalo Grove, IL 60089
847-808-4444

The Cigar King
8016 Lincoln Avenue
Skokie, IL 60077
708-675-2447

Iwan Ries & Co.
19 South Wabash Avenue
Chicago, IL 60603
312-372-1306

Jon's Pipe Shop
Kersey Callaghan, Inc.
509 East Green
Champaign, IL 61820
217-344-3459

Old Chicago Smoke Shop
3310 West Devon
Lincolnwood, IL 60659
847-679-5577

Parkwest Liquor & Smoke
Shop
2581 North Lincoln Avenue
Chicago, IL 60614
312-935-8197

Puff-N-Stuff
2518 North Acorn Drive
Round Lake Beach, IL 60073
708-265-9269

Smoker's Haven
15806 South Harlem Avenue
Orland Park, IL 60462
708-633-8331

Smokey Bear
8701 South Kedzie Avenue
Evergreen, IL 60642
708-499-0222

Strictly Men Pipe and
Tobacco Shop
13 River Oaks Drive
Calumet City, IL 60409
708-868-1088

147

The Tinder Box (#211)
1462 Fox Valley Center
Aurora, IL 60504
708-898-9450

Tinder Box/Davis Enterprises
R.C. Davis Enterprises, Inc.
1034 Louis Joliet Mall
Joliet, IL 60435
815-439-1190

Toolland, Inc.
417 West Railroad Avenue
Round Lake, IL 60073
708-5646-6222

Treasure Island Foods
302 West Illinois
#2216
Chicago, IL 60610
312-494-1500

Up Down Tobacco Shop
1550 North Wells Street
Chicago, IL 60603
312-337-8505

INDIANA

Barbara's Gift Shop
120 Main Street
Vincennes, IN 47591
812-882-1792

Briar & Bean
Box 121, Eastland Mall
800 North Green River Road
Evansville, IN 47715
812-479-8736

El Ropo Cigars, Inc.
College Mall
2969 East Third Street
Bloomington, IN 47401
812-332-3300

Men's Toy Shop, Inc.
P.O. Box 322
Old Colonial Building
Nashville, IN 47448
812-988-6590

Pipe Puffer Smoke Shop
8702 Keystone Crossing
Indianapolis, IN 46240
317-846-7473

Riegel's Pipe & Tobacco Shop
624 South Calhoun Street
Fort Wayne, IN 46802
219-422-1380

The Tinder Box (#205)
Washington Square S/C
#480
10202 East Washington
Street
Indianapolis, IN 46229
317-899-2811

The Tinder Box (#273)
110 University Park Mall
Mishawaka, IN 46545
219-277-3440

Tobacco Outlet
50532 U.S. 33 North
South Bend, IN 46637
219-277-7958

The Tobacco Shop
Lafayette Square Mall
3919 Lafayette Road
Indianapolis, IN 462654
317-299-6010

Wabash Cigar Store, Inc.
815 Wabash Avenue
Terre Haute, IN 47807
812-232-1249

IOWA

David's Briar Shoppe
944 Merle Hay Mall
Des Moines, IA 50310
515-278-8701

Tobacco Bowl
Westdale Mall
Cedar Rapids, IA 52404
319-396-3533

KANSAS

Bright Leaf
7700 East Kellogg
Wichita, KS 67207
316-685-8269

Churchill's
1801 SW Wanamaker
Topeka, KS 66604
913-273-0102

Cigar & Tabac, Ltd.
6930 West 105th
Overland Park, KS 66212
913-381-5597

Doug & George's Pipe Shop
727 Massachusetts Street
Lawrence, KS 66044
913-865-1554

Hall's Food Mart
704 Main Street
Galena, KS 66739
316-787-5006

McColla Enterprises, Ltd.
Street Corner News
2945 SW Wanamaker
Suite C
Topeka, KS 66614
913-272-8529

KENTUCKY

Adler Tobacco Co., Inc.
P.O. Box 20485
Louisville, KY 40250
502-495-3286

Kentuckiana Leased Departments, Inc.
3477 Cane Run Road
Louisville, KY 40211
502-778-7717

Kremer's Smoke Shoppe, Inc.
333 South Preston Street
Louisville, KY 40202
502-584-3332

Oxmoor Smoke Shoppe
Oxmoor Center
7900 Shelbyville Road
Louisville, KY 40222
502-426-4706

The Tobacco Barn
5023 Hinkleville Road
Paducah, KY 42001
502-442-7633

Tobacco 'N' Book Nook
Danville Manor Shopping
Center
Danville, KY 40422
606-236-READ

Up In Smoke Cigar Shop
1431 Bardstown Road
Louisville, KY 40204
502-451-1118

LOUISIANA

The Cigar Merchant L.L.C.
1001 Coolidge Boulevard
Lafayette, LA 70503
318-233-9611

Dos Jefes
5700 Magazine Street
New Orleans, LA 70115
504-899-3030

Jewel Caters
201 North New Hampshire
Covington, LA 70433
504-892-5746

M.A.'s Smoke House
1736 East 70th Street
Shreveport, LA 71105
318-797-3138

148

Phillip's Bayou Humidor
1152 South Acadian
  Thruway
Baton Rouge, LA 70806
504-353-1152

Shop-A-Lot
2707 Hazel Street
Lake Charles, LA 70601
318-433-2846

Tinder Box (#261)
Lakeside Shopping Center
3301 Veterans Memorial
  Boulevard
Metairie, LA 70002
504-242-2846

Tobacco Plus
115 East 1st Street
Crowley, LA 70527
318-783-8696

Tobacco Warehouse
P.O. Box 752
Natchitoches, LA 71458
318-352-0267

MAINE

Day's News
143 Maine Street
Brunswick, ME 04011
207-729-3131

MARYLAND

A. Fader & Son
107 East Baltimore Street
Baltimore, MD
410-685-5511

Block Arcade
213 Berry Vine Drive
Owings Mills, MD 21117
410-727-3994

Carrollton Boardwalk
7748 Riverdale Road
New Carrollton, MD 20784
301-577-8808

Decker's Inc.
401 Baltimore Pike
Bel Air, MD 21014
410-879-4400

J.B. Sims Fine Tobacco
4914 Street Elmo Avenue
Bethesda, MD 20814
301-656-7123

**Kings Contrivance Liquor
  Shop**
8630 Guilford Road
Columbia, MD 21046
410-290-7860

Lynn Roberts Company
3721 Eastern Avenue
Bethesda, MD 21224
410-551-3131

**Rolling Road Tobacco
  Warehouse, Inc.**
1420 York Road
Lutherville, MD 21093
410-339-7072

Valley Tobacco Co.
Hunt Valley Mall
Shawan Road
Cockeysville, MD 21030
410-771-3493

MASSACHUSETTS

The Cigar Emporium
Suite 300
800 Turnpike Street
North Andover, MA 01845
508-686-3000

David P. Ehrlich Co.
32 Tremont
Boston, MA 02108
617-227-1720

Gateway News
7 Washington Street
Wellesley, MA 02181
617-235-4753

Heights News & Cigar Pit
1006 Bennington Street
East Boston, MA 02128
617-569-4450**KB Tobacco**
168 Everett Avenue
Chelsea, MA 02150
617-889-0012

L.J. Peretti Co., Inc.
2½ Park Square
Boston, MA 02116
617-482-0218

The Owl Shop
416 Main Street
Worcester, MA 01608
508-753-0423

Phoenix Tobacconist
1676 Main Street
Springfield, MA 01103
413-731-8322

Pipe Rack
1247 Centre Street
Newton Centre, MA 02159
617-969-3734

The Tobacco Barn
49 Elm Street
Westfield, MA 01085
413-568-7286

**Tobacco Shed–
  Framingham**
400 Cochituate Road
Framingham, MA 01701
508-875-9851

Two Guys Smoke Shop
262 Meridian Street
East Boston, MA 02128
617-569-4450

MICHIGAN

BDT Pipe and Tobacco
21623 Jon Road
Hazel Park, MI 48030
810-542-6110

B & R Discount Center
3101 Woodward Avenue
Detroit, MI 48201
313-833-2359

Canvasbacks, Inc.
7503 South U.S. 31
Petoskey, MI 49770
616-348-5808

Churchills Ltd.
142 South Woodward
  Avenue
Birmingham, MI 48009
810-647-4555

Churchill's Ltd.
3250 West Big Beaver #330
Troy MI 48098
810-816-0740

Dearborn Tobacco Co.
22085 Michigan Avenue
Dearborn, MI 48124
313-526-1221

Dream Factory
10610 East Grand River
Brighton, MI 48116
810-227-5809

Hayes Market
VIP Discount Fine Cigars
22580 Telegraph Road
Southfield, MI 48034
810-352-2216

**Hill & Hill Tobacconists
  Ltd.**
19529 Mack Avenue
Grosse Pointe Woods, MI
  48236
313-882-9452

Hostetter's News Agency
135 Washington Avenue
Grand Haven, MI 49417
616-842-3920

149

Humidor One Panache
20000 West Ten Mile Road
Southfield, MI 48075
810-356-4600

Lil' Havana
6690-A Orchard Lake Road
West Bloomfield, MI 48322
810-539-0190

**Maison Edwards
Tobacconist**
11 Nickels Arcade
Ann Arbor, MI 48104
313-662-4145

Patros, Inc.
35329 Valleyforge Drive
Farmington Hills, MI 48331
810-489-5799

**Paul's Pipe Shop & Pipe
Hospital**
647 South Saginaw Street
Flint, MI 48502
810-235-0581

Smoker's Depot
10006 East Grand River
Brighton, MI 48116
810-220-2701

Smokers Express
47063 Van Dyke
Shelby, MI 48317
810-254-7272

Smoker's Outlet
18655 Ten Mile Road
Roseville, MI 48066
810-772-3999

Smoker's Palace
1045 Summit Street
Lapeer, MI 48446
313-664-2020

**Smoky's Cigarettes &
Cigars**
2727 South Worward
Berkley, MI 48072
810-546-8431

The Station
25940 Michigan Avenue
Inkster, MI 48141
313-561-7969

Tiffany, Inc.
1714 West Main Street
Kalamazoo, MI 49006
616-381-1414

The Tinder Box
Crossroads Mall
6650 South Westnedge
Kalamazoo, MI 49002
616-327-3447

Tobacco Emporium
2981 East Big Beaver
Troy, MI 48083
810-689-1840

Tuttle's
3835 28th Street SE
Grand Rapids, MI 49512
616-942-6990

Vintage Wine Shop
4137 Orchard Lake Road
Orchard Lake, MI 48323
810-626-3235

Apollo Liquor
1513 12th Street SE
Rochester, MN 55904
507-281-0888

F.S. Tobacco
3320 East 41st Street
Minneaplis, MN 55406
612-729-7949

Golden Leaf Ltd.
Calhoun Square
3001 Hennepin Avenue
South
Minneapolis, MN 55402
612-333-1315

Lewis Pipe & Tobacco
White Horse Pipe Co.
512 Nicollet Mall
Minneapolis, MN 55402
612-332-9139

**Mad Hatters of
Minneapolis, Inc.**
3723 Minnehaha Avenue
Minneapolis, MN 55406
612-729-7949

Surdyk, Inc.
303 East Hennepin Avenue
Minneapolis, MN 55414
612-379-3232

Tobacco Road, Inc.
831 Marquette Avenue
Minneapolis, MN 55402
612-332-9129

Cigarette Mart, Inc.
P.O. Box 1374
728 South Gloster Street
Tupelo, MS 38802
601-840-3349

Dyre-Kent Drug Co.
109 First Street
P.O. Box 100
Grenada, MS 38901
601-226-5232

The Epitome
2600 Beach Boulevard
Biloxi, MS 39531
601-388-2022

**Gautier Pharmacy Gift
Gallery**
P.O. Box 349
Gautier, MS 39553
601-497-4224

Briars and Blends
6008 Hampton Avenue
St. Louis, MO 63109
314-351-1131

Discount Smoke Shop
4807 North Lindbergh
Bridgeton, MO
314-731-7568

Fred Diebel, Tobacconist
462 Ward Parkway
Kansas City, MO 64112
816-931-2988

His/Sherlocks
Center Court
North Park Mall
Joplin, MO 64801
417-781-6345

H.S.B. Tobacconist
6362 Delmar
St. Louis, MO 63130
314-721-1483

Just For Him
1328 East Battlefield
Springfield, MO 65804
417-886-8380

The Nostalgia Shop
819 East Walnut
Colombia, MO 65201
314-874-1950

The Smoke Shop
655 Jeffco Boulevard
Arnold, MO 63010
314-296-3402

The Tinder Box (#196)
Jamestown Mall
A-168
Florissant, MO 63034
314-741-0899

Tobacco Lane
265 West Park Mall
Cape Girardeau, MO 63701
314-651-3414

**Town and Country
Tobacco**
13933 Manchester
St. Louis, MO 63011
314-227-0707

Welcome Smokers, Inc.
12984 Musket Court
St. Louis, MO 63146
314-878-6615

David's Briar Shop
Westroads Suite 3337
10000 California Street
Omaha, NE 68114
402-397-4760

Nickleby's Smoke Ring
2464 South 120th Street
Omaha, NE 68144
402-330-4556

Ted's Tobacco
Wards–#2 Gateway
Lincoln, NE 68505
402-467-3350

Churchill's Tobacco Emporium
3144 North Rainbow Boulevard
Las Vegas, NV 89108
702-645-1047

Ed's Pipes, Tobacco & Gifts
Maryland Square
3661 South Maryland Parkway, Suite 15-N
Las Vegas, NV 89109
702-734-1931

Las Vegas Paiute Tribe
1225 North Main Street
Las Vegas, NV 89101
702-387-6433

Royal Cigar Society
3900 South Paradise Road
Las Vegas, NV 89109
702-732-4411

Gold Leaf Tobacconist
920 Lafayette Road
Seabrook, NH 03874
603-474-7744

Newsshop
145 Heritage Avenue
Portsmouth, NH 03801
603-431-2020

Post Time Beer & Smoke
375 South Broadway
Salem, NH
603-898-3704

A Little Taste of Cuba
70 Witherspoon Street
Princeton, NJ 08542
609-683-8988

Cigar Cafe
44 Morris Street
Morristown, NJ 07960
201-784-3859

The Cigar Room
200 Main Street
Fort Lee, NJ 07024
201-947-5835

Cigars Plus
2140-1 Route 88
Bricktown, NJ 08753
908-295-9795

Clinton Wine & Spirits
57 Laneco Plaza
Clinton, NJ 08809
908-735-9655

Cubal Aliados Cigars, Inc.
329 48th Street
Union City, NJ 07087
201-348-0189

Globe Vending Co., Inc.
201 West Decatur Avenue
Pleasantville, NJ 08232
609-641-7811

King Tobacco
John David Ltd.
453 Menlo Park Mall
Edison, NJ 08837
908-494-8333

Northfield News & Tobacco
Route 9 and Tilton Road
Northfield, NJ 08225
609-641-9112

The Smoke Shop
235 Hudson Street
Hoboken, NJ 07030
201-217-1701

Thee Tobacco Store
405 Bloomfield Avenue
Verona, NJ 07044
201-857-2266

The Tobacco Shop, Inc.
12 Chestnut Street
Ridgewood, NJ 07450
201-447-2204

Track Town Smoke Shop
2111 Route 70 West
Cherry Hill, NJ 08002
609-662-0214

United Card & Smoke Shop
13 Broadway
Denville, NJ 07834
201-627-6718

Lucas Pipe & Tobacco
201 East University
Las Cruces, NM 88001
505-526-3411

Pueblo Pipe Shop
2685 Louisiana NE
Albuquerque, NM 87110
505-881-7999

Santa Fe Cigar Co.
518 Old Santa Fe Trail
Suite 3
Santa Fe, NM 87501
505-982-1044

Smoke Shop
1308 Pope Street
Silver City, NM 88061
505-388-5575

Strollers Palace Cigar
7 Montoya Circle
Santa Fe, NM 87501
505-988-3739

Tobacco Tin
700 South Telshor
#1092
Las Cruces, NM 88001
505-526-3411

Alfred Dunhill of London, Inc.
450 Park Avenue
Mezzanine Level
New York, NY 10022
212-888-4000

Arnold's Tobacco Shop
323 Madison Avenue
New York, NY 10017
212-697-1477

Barclay-Rex Pipe Shop, Inc.
7 Maiden Lane
New York, NY 10038
212-962-3355

Barney's Court Cut Rate
76 Court Str.
Brooklyn, NY 11201
718-875-8355

Bellezia Tobacco Shop
4549 Main Street
Snyder, NY 14226
716-839-5381

Cigar Landing
89 Fulton Street
Pier 17–South Street Seaport
New York, NY 10038
800-976-6535

De La Concha Tobacconist
1390 Avenue of the Americas
New York, NY 10019
212-757-3167

Edleez Tobacco, Inc.
Stuyvesant Plaza
Albany, NY 12203
518-489-6872

Edleez West
4 West Main Street
Fredonia, NY 14063
716-672-4470

Famous Smoke Shop
55 West 39th Street
New York, NY 10018
212-221-1408

Fortune Smoke Shop
527 Old Country Road
Westbury, NY 11590
516-997-8109

The Gift Source
90-15 Queens Boulevard
Elmhurst, NY 11373
718-592-0400

Hero's Smoke Inc.
517 A East Jerico Turnpike
Huntington Station, NY
   11746
516-351-7131

House of Oxford
   Distributors
172 5th Avenue
New York, NY 10010
212-243-1943

Japan Trade Center
Smoking Articles Section
1221 Avenue of the Americas
New York, NY 10020
212-977-0449

JeLomax Corp.
1 Whitehall Street
New York, NY 10004
212-425-0198

Kieffer's Cigar Store
851 North Salina Street
Syracuse, NY 13208
315-475-3988

Lindy's Smoke Shop
260 Sunrise Highway
Lindenhurst, NY 11757
516-957-0287

Maxis Smoke Shop
253-22 Union Turnpike
Floral Park, NY 11004
718-234-5000

Market Place Smoke Shop,
   Inc.
4924 Spring Valley Market
   Place
Spring Valley, NY 10977
914-356-3717

Mom's Cigars, Inc.
J.R. Tobacco
1119 Central Park Avenue
Scarsdale, NY 10583
914-723-3088

Nat Sherman, Inc.
500 Fifth Avenue
New York, NY 10110
212-246-5500

Nyack Tobacco Co., Inc.
169 Burd Street
Nyack, NY 10960
914-353-9230

Puff and Stuff
161-10 Northern Boulevard
Flushing, NY 11358
718-321-3908

S.C. Pipes of Canada
P.O. Box 451
Chateaugay, NY 12920
514-264-6123

Shree Pranam Tobacco
114 Liberty Street
New York, NY 10006
212-406-3106

Smoke Stax
412 Hillside Avenue
New Hyde Park, NY 11040
516-355-0915

Tinder Box #362
8212 Transit Road
K-Mart Plaza
Williamsville, NY 14221
716-689-2914

Tobacco & Gift Emporium
3277 Richmond Avenue
Staten Island, NY 10312
718-948-2899

Tobacco Plaza, Ltd.
80 Northern Boulevard
Great Neck, NY 11021
516-829-7134

United Smoke Shop
2 East Market Street
Snyder, NY 14226
716-839-5381

W.E. Brown Co.
6 West Market Street
Corning, NY 14830
607-962-2612

Wine Enthusiast Wine
   Cellars & Unique Gifts
8 Saw Mill River Road
Hawthorne, NY 10532
914-345-9463

Wolcott's Beverage &
   Tobacco Co.
1007 Union Center Highway
Endicott, NY 13760
607-754-0246

Anstead's Tobacco
337 Cross Creek Mall
Fayetteville, NC 28303
910-864-5705

Gilreath Tobacco Co., Inc.
Pleasures & Treasures
221 Four Seasons Town
   Centre
Greensboro, NC 27407
919-855-1301

Infinity's End, Inc.
3704 East Independence
   Boulevard
Charlotte, NC 28205
704-535-1710

Island Tobacco Co.
P.O. Box 1972
Nags Head, NC 27959
919-441-1392

McCranie's Pipe Shop
4143 Park Road
Park Road Shopping Center
Charlotte, NC 28209
704-523-8554

Pipes by George
1209 Hillsborough Street
Raleigh, NC 27603
919-829-1167

Pipes Ltd.
174 Valley Hills Mall
Hickory, NC
704-328-8002

Ruptured Moon
774 4th Street Drive SW
Hickory, NC 28602
704-324-6969

Sir Toms Tobacco
Emporium
129 West 4th Avenue
Hendersonville, NC 28792
704-697-7753

The Smoke Stack
1010 North Cedar Street
Lumberton, NC 28358
910-738-7158

Smokey Joe's Inc.
145 Ebenezer Lane
Statesville, NC 28677
704-876-0690

The Tinder Box (#178)
Crabtree Valley Mall
4325 Glenwood Avenue
Raleigh, NC 27612
919-787-1310

The Tinder Box (#208)
South Park Shopping Center
4400 Sharon Road
Charlotte, NC 28209
704-523-8554

The Tinder Box (#237)
3320 Silas Creek Parkway
Suite 208 - Hanes Mall
Winston-Salem, NC 27103
919-765-9511

Tobacconists of Raleigh
3901 Capitol Boulevard
Suite 171
Raleigh, NC 27604
919-954-0020

OHIO

Barclay Pipe & Tobacco
1677 West Lane Avenue
M-12
Columbus, OH 43221
614-486-4243

City News
135 South Market Street
Wooster, OH 44691
216-262-5151

City News
100 North Main Street
Mansfield, OH 44902
419-524-0261

Cousin's Cigar Co.
1828 Euclid Avenue
Cleveland, OH 44115
216-781-9390

The Cupboard
2613 Vine Street
Cincinnati, OH 45219
513-281-8110

Doc's Smoke Shop
12 West Mulberry Street
Lebanon, OH 45036
513-932-9939

Downtown Tobacco
44 Public Square
Medina, OH 44256
216-722-9096

Duncan Hill, Ltd.
Park Center
7245 Whipple Avenue NW
North Canton, OH 44720
216-494-2323

Girard Book & News
101 North State Street
Girard, OH 44420-2594
216-545-8356

Humidor Plus
6157 Cleveland Avenue
Columbus, OH 43231
614-891-9463

Jo Vann's Inc.
1483 Som Center
Mayfield Heights, OH 44124
216-442-4755

The Pipe Rack
2200 Manchester Road
Akron, OH 44314
216-745-9022

Prime Pharmacy Group,
Inc.
1510 Gallia Street
Portsmouth, OH 45662
614-353-7356

Smoker's Haven
17 South High Street
Columbus, OH 43215
614-469-1028

Smoker's Inn/Port Royale
3301 West Central Avenue
Toledo, OH 43606
419-537-1491

Straus Tobacconist
410 Walnut Street
Cincinnati, OH 45202
513-621-3388

The Tinder Box #157
2700 Miamisburg-
Centerville Road
Dayton, OH 45459
513-433-2841

The Tinder Box #228
4236 West Land Mall
Columbus, OH 43228
614-276-2904

The Tinder Box #279
434 Great Northern Mall
North Olmsted, OH 44070
216-572-3668

The Tobacco Pouch
26 North Main Street
Chagrin Falls, OH 44022
216-247-5365

The Wild Berry
15 West High Street
Oxford, OH 45056
513-523-4345

OKLAHOMA

ABC Store
4508 South May
Oklahoma City, OK 73119
405-685-1716

Potawatomi Tribal Store
1901 South Gordon Cooper
Drive
Shawnee, OK 74801
405-275-1480

Ted's Pipe Shop, Ltd.
2002 Utica Square
Tulsa, OK 74114
918-742-4996

Tobacco Exchange
2828 NW 63rd Street
French Market Mall
Oklahoma City, OK 73162
405-721-0652

Zydot Unlimited, Inc.
3105 East Skelly Drive
Suite 412
Tulsa, OK 74105
918-747-2400

OREGON

82nd Avenue Tobacco &
Pipe
400 SE 82nd Avenue
Portland, OR 97216
503-255-9987

Cascade News & Tobacco
11103 SE Main
Milwaukie, OR 97222
503-786-3607

Eclipse Gifts
P.O. Box 2554
Eugene, OR 97402
503-484-7198

Forest Grove Tobacco
3034 Pacific Avenue
Forest Grove, OR 97116
503-359-9240

Hunky Dory Pipe and Tobacco
293 West 7th Avenue
Eugene, OR 97401
503-345-1853

News & Smokes
1330 NW 6th Street
Grants Pass, OR 97526
503-479-7506

Paul's–Mall 205
9986 SE Washington Street
Portland, OR 97216
503-255-4471

Rich's Cigar Store
801 SW Alder Street
Portland, OR 97205
503-228-1700

Timber Valley Tobaccos
3355 SW Cedar Hills Boulevard
Beaverton, OR 97005
503-644-3837

The Tinder Box (#166)
Jantzen Beach Center
1615 Jantzen Beach Center
Portland, OR 97217
503-283-4924

T. Whittaker Tobaccos
7276 SW Beav-Hill Hgwy
Suite 269
Portland, OR 97225
503-246-1894

PENNSYLVANIA

Artifax
2446 Cottman Avenue
Philadelphia, PA 19149
215-331-0306

Burdick's Hatboro News Agency
206 South York Road
Hatboro, PA 19040
215-675-9960

Capital Cigars
919 Susquehanna Street
Harrisburg, PA 17102
717-233-4149

Capricorn Tobacco, Inc.
1518 Sansom Street
Philadelphia, PA 19102
215-563-9850

Custom Blends Tobacco & News
2559 South Queen Street
York, PA 17402
717-741-4972

Father's Tobacco
1235 Quentin Road
Lebanon Plaza Mall
Lebanon, PA 17042
717-273-3666

Hain's Pipe Shop
225 South George Street
York, PA 17403
717-843-2237

Holt's Cigar Co., Inc.
2901 Grant Avenue
Philadelphia, PA 19114
215-676-8778

Jerningan's Enterprises, Inc.
147 Monroeville Mall
Monroeville, PA 15146
412-531-5881

Klafter's, Inc.
Cigarette Express
216 North Beaver Street
New Castle, PA 16101
412-658-6561

Magikal Garden
1174 Wyoming Avenue
Exeter, PA 18643
217-655-0924

Markowitz Bros.
256 Wyoming Avenue
Scranton, PA 18503
717-342-0315

Montage Tobacco Co.
623 Davis Street
Scranton, PA 18505
717-342-3388

Pittston Candy & Cigar Co.
197 Broad Street
Pittston, PA 18640
717-883-1050

Poor Richard's
Freight House Shops
Station Square
Pittsburgh, PA 15219
412-281-1133

Tinder Box #364
393 West Lancaster Avenue
Haverford, PA 19041
610-896-4511

The Tobacco Barn
348 North 9th Street
Stroudsburg, PA 18360
717-424-0938

Tobacco Country Inc.
107 Neshaminy Mall
Bensalem, PA 19020
215-357-6615

Tobacco Mart
900 Market Street
Lemoyne, PA 17043
717-975-0994

Tobacco Village
598 Whitehall Mall
Whitehall, PA 18052
215-264-5371

Tobacco Village
North East Plaza
7300 Bustleton Avenue
Philadelphia, PA 19152
215-745-7040

United Cut Rate Store/Tobacco Outlets
19 East Bridge Street
Morrisville, PA 19067
215-295-3835

Wooden Indian Tobacco Shop
Manoa Shopping Center
Havertown, PA 19083
610-449-7001

Fun Times Dist. Co.
P.O. Box 361288
San Juan, PR 00936
809-788-3588

Good Times Smoke Shop
McKinley #74 Oeste
Mayaguez, PR 00680
809-265-2380

International House of Cigars
PMC Box 176
B-2 Calle Tabonuco
Guaynabo, PR 00968
809-782-6871

Pepin's
Fatima #5, URB Palmar Sur
Carolina, PR 00979
809-792-1591

The Smoker's Suite, Inc.
Hotel San Juan and Casino
La Galera Avenue, Isla Verde
Carolina, PR 00979
809-781-4584

Humidor Tobacco
1500 Oaklawn Avenue
Cranston, RI 02920
401-463-5949

Jolly Roger Smokeshop
2009 C Smith Street
North Providence, RI 02911
401-231-7270

**Red Carpet Smoke Shop,
Incorporated**
108½ Waterman Street
Providence, RI 02906
401-421-4499

Boda Pipes, ACF Inc.
McAlister Square Mall
225 South Pleasantburg
  Drive
Greenville, SC 29607
803-242-1545

Intermezzo
2015 Devine Street
Columbia, SC 29205
803-799-2276

Pipe Dreams
2441 Whiskey Road South
Aiken Mall
Aiken, SC 29803
803-642-0080

The Smoke Stack Ltd.
205 The Market Place
Hilton Head Island, SC
  29928
803-785-5599

The Smoking Lamp
197 East Bay Street
Charleston, SC 29401
803-577-7339

Tinder Box (#325)
Braircliffe Mall
10177 North Kings Highway
Myrtle Beach, SC 29577
803-272-2336

Eastwold Smoke Shop
136 South Phillips Avenue
Sioux Falls, SD 57102
605-332-2071

ARA Discount Tobacco Inc.
901-C Hollywood Drive
Jackson, TN 38301
901-423-4811

Arcade Smoke Shop
11 Arcade
Nashville, TN 37219
615-726-8031

Briar & Bean
Unit 280
Governor's Square Mall
Clarksville, TN 37040
615-552-6465

**The Chattanooga Billiard
Club**
110 Jordan Drive
Chattanooga, TN 37421
615-499-8637

**Elliston Place Pipe &
Tobacco Shop**
2204-H Elliston Place
Nashville, TN 37203
615-320-7624

Fred Stoker & Sons
Route 1
PO Box 707
Dresden, TN 38225
901-364-5419

**G.B. Tobacco Company,
Inc.**
603 Skyline Drive
Gatlinburg, TN 37738
615-436-4412

Jim's Pipes and Gifts
6925-B Maynardville
  Highway
Knoxville, TN 37918
615-922-3914

Mosko's Inc.
2204 Elliston Place
Nashville, TN 37203
615-327-2658

Smokin' Joe's
6110 Papermill Road
Knoxville, TN 37922
615-584-9010

Smoky's Pipe and Tobacco
143 Montvue Center
Knoxville, TN 37919
615-693-8371

Three Ten Pipe & Tobacco
109 East Main Street
Murfreesboro, TN 37130
615-893-3100

The Tinder Box (#310)
4477 Mall of Memphis
  Suite 2
Memphis, TN 38118
901-795-0360

Tobacco Corner Ltd.
669 South Mendenhall
Memphis, TN 38117
901-682-3326

Tobacco Mart
AVM & HMV & AP Corp.
4850 Highway 58
Chattanooga, TN 37416
615-855-6818

Tobacco Road Smoke Shop
Harding Mall
4050 Nolensville Road
Nashville, TN 37211
615-331-7139

Uptown's Smoke Shop
P.O. Box 110710
Nashville, TN 37222
615-331-8041

Amy Lynn, Inc.
5800 Maple Avenue
Dallas, TX 75235
214-350-2488

Antique Pipe Shoppe
6366 Richmond Avenue
Houston, TX 77057
713-785-4080

Avalon Liquor
Fine Wines & Beer
2880 Westheimer
Houston, TX 77098
713-520-5550

Beverage City #2
11411 R
North Central Expressway
Dallas, TX 75243
214-750-9313

The Beverage Shop
4755 West Panther Creek
  Drive
The Woodlands, TX 77381
713-363-9463

B.R. News
506 West 33rd Street
Austin, TX 78705
512-454-9110

The Briar Shoppe
2412 Times Boulevard
Houston, TX 77005
713-529-6347

Capitol City Distributing
9411 North IH 35
Austin, TX 78753
512-837-5337

Casa Petrides Tobacco
306 South Broadway
McAllen, TX 78501
210-631-5219

Cigar Palace
121 West 8th Street
Austin, TX 78701
512- 472-2277

155

Cigars, Pipes & More, Inc.
14520 Memorial Drive #22
Houston, TX 77079
713-493-9196

D's Pipes Etc.
200 North 15th Street
Corsicana, TX 75110
903-874-8661

Don's Humidor
1412 North Valley Mills
Drive
Waco, TX 76710
817-772-3919

Edward's Pipe & Cigar
1715 Promenade Center
Richardson, TX 75080
214-669-3087

Greenway Pipe & Tobacco
5 Greenway Plaza East
Suite C-4
Houston, TX 77046
713-626-1636

Hill Country Humidor
122 North LBJ Drive
San Marcos, TX 78666
512-396-7473

Hollywood Tobacco Shop
1660 Westheimer
Houston, TX 77006
713-528-3234

The Humidor, Inc.
6900 San Pedro
Suite 111
San Antonio, TX 78216
210-824-1209

Jeffrey Stone Pipe Shoppe, Inc.
9694 Westheimer
Houston, TX 77063
713-783-3555

Lone Star Cigars
13305 Montfort Drive
Dallas, TX 75240
214-392-4427

Lone Star Tobacco, Inc.
3741 FM 1960 West
Houston, TX 77068
713-444-2464

McCoy's Fine Cigars & Tobaccos
1201 Louisiana
#B-204
Houston, TX 77002
713-739-8110

Oat Willies
617 West 29th Street
Austin, TX 78705
512- 454-9110

Paradise Gifts
1200 McKinnney #481
Houston, TX 77010
713-650-8708

Pipe Dreams
4706 Maple Avenue
Dallas, TX 75219
214-520-8000

Pipes Plus
504 West 4th Street
Austin, TX 78705
512- 478-7236

Pipe World, Inc.
2160 Highland Mall
Austin, TX 78752
512-451-3713

Puff n' Stuff
107 Hulen Mall
Fort Worth, TX 76132
817-294-0600

Richard's Liquors
P.O. Box 130488
Houston, TX 77219
713-783-3344

Ruta Maya Tobacco
218 West 4th Street
Austin, TX 78701
512- 472-9637

Smoke-N-Toke
9376-C Richmond Avenue
Houston, TX 77063
713-781-1179

The Smoke Shop
30 Western Plaza
Amarillo, TX 79109
806-353-6331

Smoker's Discount #8
3266 South 14th Street
Abilene, TX 79605
915-695-4414

Smoker's Haven
1915 19th Street
Lubbock, TX 79405
806-744-0017

Smokin J's Discount Tobacco
907 Sundown Highway
Levelland, TX 79336
806-894-2847

TJ's Catering and Take Out
2901 Wilcrest No. 137
Houston, TX 77042
713-974-5442

Tobacco Bowl of Texas, Inc.
622 NW Loop 410
Suite 276
San Antonio, TX 78216
210-349-7708

Tobacco Club
4043 Trinity Mills
Suite 112
Dallas, TX 75287
214-306-2880

Tobacco Lane I
2911 East Division–318
Arlington, TX 76011
817-640-3210

Tobacco Lane
2201 I-35 East South
Golden Triangle Mall P-9
Denton, TX 76205
817-566-6421

Tobacco Lane
2220 NE Mall
Hurst, TX 76053
817-284-7251

Tobacco World
Promenade
1220 Airline Road
Suite 270
Corpus Christi, TX 78412
512-992-4427

Up In Smoke
3621 Irving Mall
Irving, TX 75062
214-255-8812

Very Best
9960-A Harwin Drive
Houston, TX 77036
713-975-7852

Wiggy's
1130 West 6th Street
Austin, TX 78703
512-474-9463

UTAH

Jeanie's Smoke Shop
156 South State Street
Salt Lake City, UT 84111
801-322-2817

The Tinder Box
6191 Fashion Place Mall
Murray, UT 84107
801-268-1321

The Tinder Box (#312)
Crossroads Plaza A-26
50 South Main Street
Salt Lake City, UT 84111
801-322-2817

VERMONT

Garcia Tobacco Shop
Burlington Square Mall
Burlington, VT 05401
802-658-5737

VIRGINIA

Berrane Enterprises, Inc.
2231 Route 17
Yorktown, VA 23693
804-596-7618

Cigar Club International, Inc.
2869 Duke Street
Alexandria, VA 22314
703-823-2234

Emerson Fine Tobaccos
Military Circle Center
Norfolk, VA 23502
804-461-6848

John B. Hayes, Tobacconist
11755-L Fair Oaks Mall
Fairfax, VA 22033
703-385-3033

Octopus Gardens
13626 Jefferson Davis
Highway
Woodbridge, VA 22191
703-491-6118

Pipe Collectors of America
P.O. Box 5179
Woodbridge, VA 22194
703-787-7655

**The Pipe Dream of
Alexandria, Inc.**
John Crouch Tobacconist
215 King Street
Alexandria, VA 22314
703-548-2900

Potomac Retail Ent., Inc.
1500 Wilson Boulevard
Arlington, VA 22209
703-276-7225

Tobacco Alley
120 Wilson Street
Blacksburg, VA 24060
703-951-3154

Tobacco House Ltd.
3138 West Cary Street
Richmond, VA 23221
804-353-4675

VIRGIN ISLANDS

A.H. Riise Gift & Liquor
P.O. Box 6280
St. Thomas, VI 00804
809-776-2303

Baci Duty Free
55 Company Street
Christiansted, VI 00820
809-773-5040

Jolly Roger Tobacconist Inc.
P.O. Box 302605
St. Thomas, VI 00803
809-774-2605

Steele's Smokes & Sweets
Pan Am Pavilion
1102 Strand Street, Suite 19
Christiansted, VI 00820
809-773-3366

WASHINGTON

Arcade Smoke Shop
610 Pine Street
Seattle, WA 98101
206-587-0159

**Downtown Cigar &
Premium Shop**
310 Columbia Street
Seattle, WA 98104
206-624-2794

G. & G. Cigar Co.
504 Second Avenue
Smith Tower
Seattle, WA 98104
206-623-6721

Le Bon Vie
5826 Pacific Avenue SE
Lacey, WA 98503
360-493-1454

March Point Enterprises
815 South March Point Road
Anacortes, WA 98221
360-293-5632

Mike's Smoke Shop
101 Pioneer Way East
Tacoma, WA 98404
206-627-8959

R.J. Clark
Point Roberts Tobacco
Blender–P.O. Box 312
Point Roberts, WA
98281
604-681-8021

Sir Winston & Co.
1324 Commercial Street
Bellingham, WA 98226
360-647-9241

**South Tacoma Pipe &
Tobacco**
5602 South Lawrence
Tacoma, WA 98409
206-472-4931

The Tinder Box (#168)
4502 South Steele Street
Tacoma Mall #1131
Tacoma, WA 98409
206-472-9993

The Tinder Box (#316)
10150 Main Street
Bellview, WA 98004
206-451-8544

Thomas D's Tobacco
Box 3203
Silverdale, WA 98383
206-692-0681

University Smoke Shop
4539 University Way NE
Seattle, WA 98105
206-632-8891

WEST VIRGINIA

Multi-Sound Music Corp.
3708 McCorkel Avenue SE
Charleston, WV 25304
304-925-8273

**The Squire Tobacco
Unlimited**
30 Capital Street
Charleston, WV 25301
304-345-0366

Bibliography

- Anwer Bati, *The Cigar Companion*, Running Press, Philadelphia, 1993.
- Richard Carleton Hacker, *The Ultimate Cigar Book*, Autumngold Publishing, Beverly Hills, 1993.
- Brian Innes, *The Book of the Havana Cigar*, Orbis Publishing, London, 1983.
- Richard B. Perelman, *Perelman's Pocket Cyclopedia of Cigars*, Perelman, Pioneer & Co., Los Angeles, 1995.
- Theo Rudman, *Rudman's Complete Pocket Guide to Cigars*, Good Living Publishing, Cape Town, South Africa, 1996.

Index